NATURE EXPLORERS
Michigan Wildlife:
A Coloring Field Guide

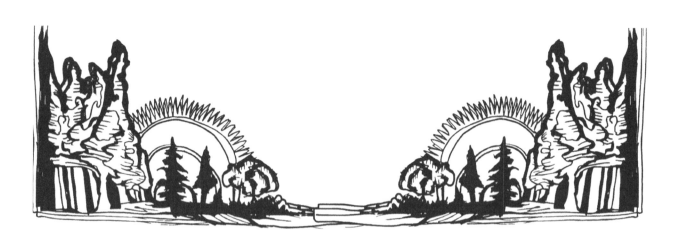

Written by Amalia Celeste Fernand

Illustrated by Patrick B. Bradley & Anna Bazyl

to: Anna
Always fi_____
6/28/19 ♡ Amalia Celeste _____

D1377398

This publication has chosen to capitalize official bird names in accordance with the system established by the International Ornithologist's Union, and recognized by the National Audubon Society.

ISBN: 069299601X
ISBN-13: 978-0692996010
Nature Explorers International, Benzonia, Michigan
 www.natureexploreresinternational.com
www.amaliaexplores.com

This field guide has been produced in collaboration with the Benzie Conservation District, and designed by Aimé Merizon, Education Outreach Coordinator.

www.benziecd.org

This book is dedicated to my students.

The more I teach, the more I learn.

Each one of you has helped me

to grow into a better educator.

CONTENTS

Introduction to Michigan.. vi

How to Use this Book.. 1

Nature Explorers Activities... 2

Introduction to Amphibians... 4

American Toad.. 6

Eastern Red-backed Salamander.. 8

Gray Tree Frog.. 10

Mudpuppy... 12

Wood Frog... 14

Amphibian Activities.. 16

Introduction to Reptiles.. 18

Common Garter Snake.. 20

Eastern Box Turtle... 22

Eastern Massasauga Rattlesnake.. 24

Painted Turtle.. 26

Snapping Turtle.. 28

Reptile Activities.. 30

Introduction to Birds.. 32

American Robin... 34

Bald Eagle.. 36

Barred Owl... 38

Black-capped Chickadee.. 40

Canada Goose.. 42

Pileated Woodpecker.. 44

Red-tailed Hawk.. 46

Ring-billed Gull.. 48

Ruffed Grouse.. 50

Turkey Vulture... 52

Wild Turkey.. 54

Bird Activities... 56

Introduction to Mammals.. 58

American Mink... 60

Black Bear... 62

Bobcat.. 64

Coyote.. 66

North American Porcupine... 68

Northern Raccoon.. 70

Northern River Otter... 72

Red Fox... 74

Virgina Opossum... 76

White-tailed Deer.. 78

Mammal Activities... 80

Species Checklists.. 82

Nature Knowledge Dictionary.. 89

Acknowledgments.. 95

References... 97

INTRODUCTION

Michigan is a distinctive state in the northern United States of America. It borders Canada, and is made up of two peninsulas that are surrounded by four of the five Great Lakes. The Lower Peninsula is shaped like a mitten and recognizable from outer space. In the Upper and Lower Peninsulas of Michigan combined, there are over 3,300 miles of shoreline along some of the largest freshwater lakes in the world.

Forested islands, extensive beaches, and giant sand dunes lead to hundreds of miles of streams and rivers, thousands of inland lakes, and both evergreen and deciduous forests. The variety of habitats, abundance of fresh water, and large areas of woodlands in Michigan make it an excellent place to view wildlife. Use this book as a guide to help you learn about both common and unique Michigan animals.

To find Michigan on a globe, look for the Great Lakes in North America.

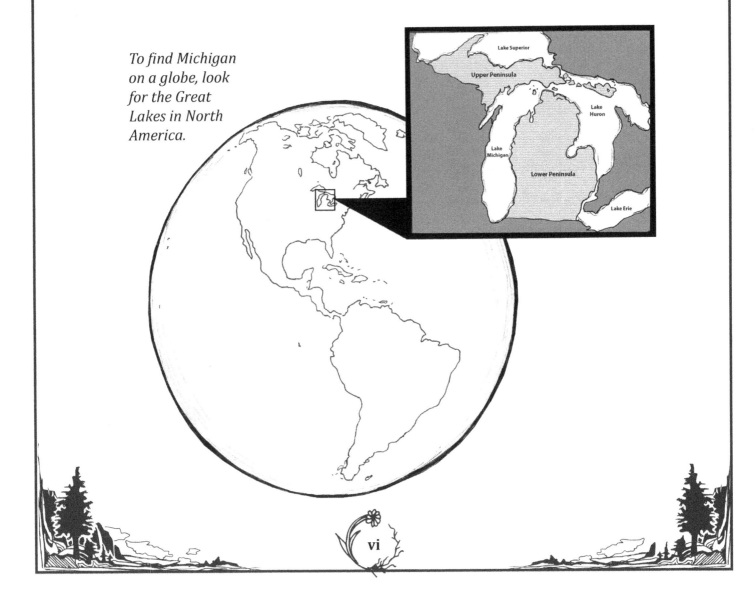

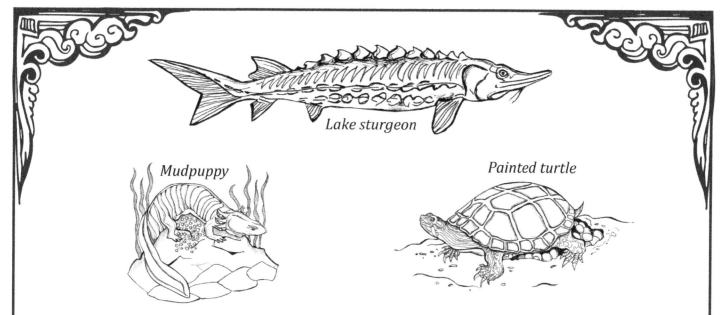

Lake sturgeon

Mudpuppy

Painted turtle

All animals can be divided into two groups: vertebrates and invertebrates. Vertebrates have backbones and invertebrates do not. There are five main classes of vertebrates: fish, amphibians, reptiles, birds, and mammals.

The animals in this book are divided into vertebrate groups. Nurture your nature knowledge by reading about each animal that you color. If there is a word that you don't understand, check the dictionary in the back.

Find out more by looking in guidebooks, starting a species list, and using the checklists provided to make observations of the animals that you see. Complete the optional activities in each section to add art, science, and games into your life as a young naturalist.

Wild turkey

White-tailed deer

DRAW A PICTURE

Draw a picture of your favorite Michigan animal on this page. Think about where your animal lives and what it eats. A habitat is an animal's home and includes food, water, shelter, and space. Diet is what an animal eats. Herbivores only eat plants, carnivores only eat other animals, and omnivores eat both plants and meat.

HOW TO USE THIS BOOK

This field guide is divided into four main sections: amphibians, reptiles, birds, and mammals. Each section begins with introduction pages that include an outline of Michigan around the featured wildlife and ends with activity pages.

Every animal has two pages with pictures and borders for you to color. The first page includes their size, diet, habitat, and a paragraph about what they look like and how they communicate. A small map of Michigan with a shaded area shows the range of where the animal lives in the state.

The second page consists of life cycle information and cool facts. Find out how many babies they have, what they do in the winter, and their lifespan. The nature knowledge part of the page adds a variety of interesting details about each animal.

The bird section includes tracks, wingspan, and calls. In the mammals section, scat and track measurements are listed along with other natural signs.

To color your pictures like real wildlife, look at the first few sentences of their "about" paragraph for a description of their colors.

At the end of each section are two pages of Nature Explorers activities. There is an art project, a science experiment, a game, and a suggestion for outdoor exploration. Have fun with these activities at home or school!

At the end of the book are your species checklists and glossary. When you see an animal, try to identify it. Find it in your checklists and fill in the location, habitat, how many of them there are, and the date. This will help you to keep track of the times and places that you are more likely to see certain wildlife.

The amphibian, reptile, and mammal checklists include all of the species that are found in the state. The birds list includes 75 common or interesting species, and a blank space for you to write in extras.

The glossary is called a nature knowledge dictionary because it will explain what the words that you don't know mean. Learning ecological terms such as diurnal, terrestrial, and opportunistic will strengthen your naturalist understanding of the world.

Be a Nature Explorer!

MAKE ART: Nature Journal & Collection Box

- Cut two pieces of cardboard that are the same size out of cereal boxes.
- Decorate them with paint, stickers, or animal pictures from old magazines.
- Cut paper for the inside.
- Punch two holes that line up in the sheets of paper and the cover.
- String yarn through the holes and tie it loosely so that your book can open.
- Draw nature pictures in your journal and sketch tracks and scat that you find. Make leaf and bark rubbings, take notes, start a species list, and record your observations in the field.
- Make a nature collection box by decorating an old egg carton or shoe box.

PLAY GAMES: Michigan Animal Follow the Leader

Play traditional follow-the-leader with an animal twist by having the leaders pretend to be Michigan wildlife.

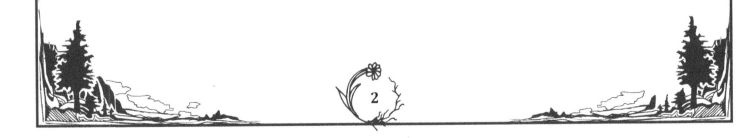

EXPERIMENT WITH SCIENCE: Scientific Method

- When writing notes in your nature journal, practice using the scientific method.
- Ask a question or think of a problem that you would like to solve.
- When you think of a guess for the answer to your question, that is called a hypothesis.
- Come up with a procedure to test your hypothesis.
- Gather materials and conduct an experiment.
- Record your observations and make a conclusion.

EXPLORE NATURE: Nature Walks

Get outside and explore nature as much as you can. You can take a nature walk anywhere! Whether it is a backyard, a schoolyard, a meadow, a forest, a beach, or a stream. When you slow down and look closely, there are always interesting things to discover in nature. Bring a magnifying glass, binoculars, a ruler, and a bug box with you if you can. Always tell an adult where you are going, and be prepared for weather with sunscreen or a raincoat.

As a Nature Explorer, it is your responsibility to respect the environment and preserve natural areas. You can learn a lot by finding interesting natural objects for your collection, but you should not pick live plants or mushrooms. Follow the rule of finding things that are: "dead, down, and brown."

Go on a bug hunt to look for invertebrates under rocks and logs, but always put the rock or log back, it is a habitat. Release any live insects or animals in the same place that you found them. Do not keep wildlife as pets.

AMPHIBIANS

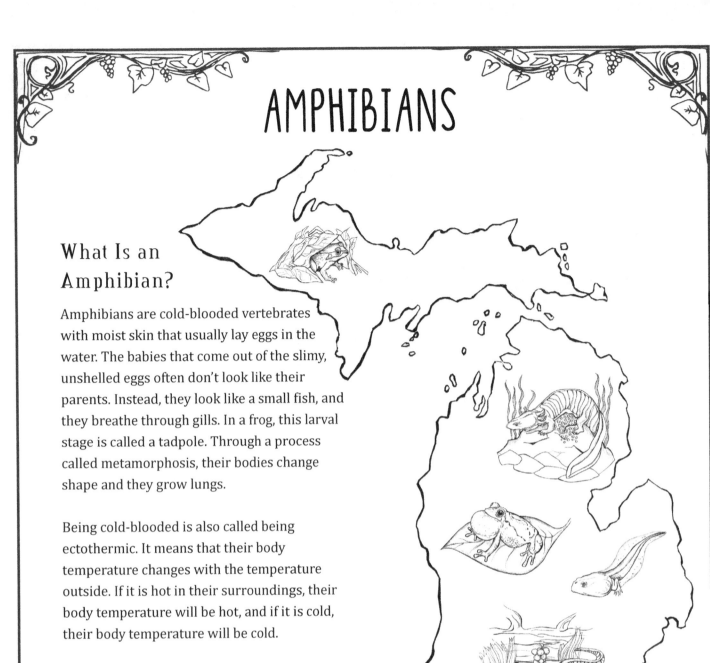

What Is an Amphibian?

Amphibians are cold-blooded vertebrates with moist skin that usually lay eggs in the water. The babies that come out of the slimy, unshelled eggs often don't look like their parents. Instead, they look like a small fish, and they breathe through gills. In a frog, this larval stage is called a tadpole. Through a process called metamorphosis, their bodies change shape and they grow lungs.

Being cold-blooded is also called being ectothermic. It means that their body temperature changes with the temperature outside. If it is hot in their surroundings, their body temperature will be hot, and if it is cold, their body temperature will be cold.

Amphibians can breathe through their absorbent skin and need fresh water to keep it moist. Amphibians are divided into three main groups: frogs, caecilians, and salamanders.

Michigan Amphibians

Michigan is home to 24 different kinds of amphibians: 13 species of frogs and 11 species of salamanders.

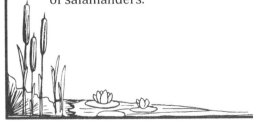

The Study of Amphibians

Biology is the study of life. Zoology is the study of animals. Herpetology is a branch of zoology that means the study of reptiles and amphibians.

Amphibian Encounters

Be careful when handling amphibians. There are some that excrete toxins that can cause a reaction in humans. Always wash your hands before and after touching amphibians. Their thin skin is very sensitive, and everyday things that we use like soap, lotion, bug-spray, and sunscreen can be harmful to them.

Amphibians are indicator species. They are important to a balanced food chain and are found in healthy ecosystems. Do not capture them to keep as pets, and do not release non-native pets into the wild.

Make a frog house in your backyard by creating a safe shelter with fresh water. Paint a terra cotta pot and lay it in a shady spot in your yard. Watch for visitors to your frog house, and learn to identify frog calls to find out what kinds of frogs live near you.

Bullfrogs are common in Michigan near bodies of water.

American Toad

(Bufo americanus)

Range

ABOUT: American toads are the most common amphibian in Michigan. Their thick bumpy skin is usually brown with black spots. The males have darker colored throats, and their call is a loud musical trill that lasts up to 30 seconds.

SIZE: Length: 2 to 4.5 in. (females are larger)

DIET: Toads are considered great garden friends. They eat thousands of invertebrates a year, including: grasshoppers, flies, spiders, and slugs. Tadpoles eat aquatic plants and carrion.

HABITAT: Terrestrial and very adaptable, they live in forests, fields, wetlands, and backyards.

LIFE CYCLE

In early spring, big groups of toads gather near shallow ponds. The females lay long strings of up to 20,000 eggs wrapped around water plants. The tadpoles hatch about a week later, and transform after 40 to 70 days. In the fall, they use their back legs as shovels to dig deep down into the dirt below the frost line. They stay very still for the entire winter, breathing slowly with a slow heart rate. Their lifespan is 5 to 8 years.

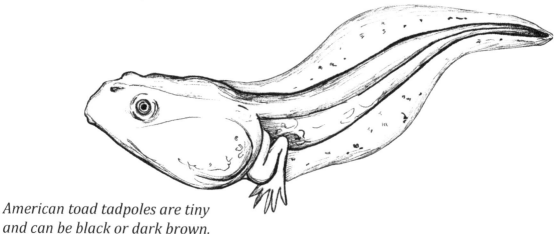

American toad tadpoles are tiny and can be black or dark brown.

NATURE KNOWLEDGE

• A toad is a kind of frog that usually lives on land. They have warty skin and short legs. Toads travel using short hops, and frogs take long leaps.

• American toads have toxins in their skin that help to protect them from predators. If you touch your eye after handling an American toad, you could have a reaction. Toads do not cause warts.

• American toads can change their skin color from light tan to dark brown depending on their environment.

• Fowler's toads look like American toads, but they are smaller with more warts, lighter colored skin, and a shorter, lower-pitched call.

Eastern Red-backed Salamander

(Plethodon cinereus)

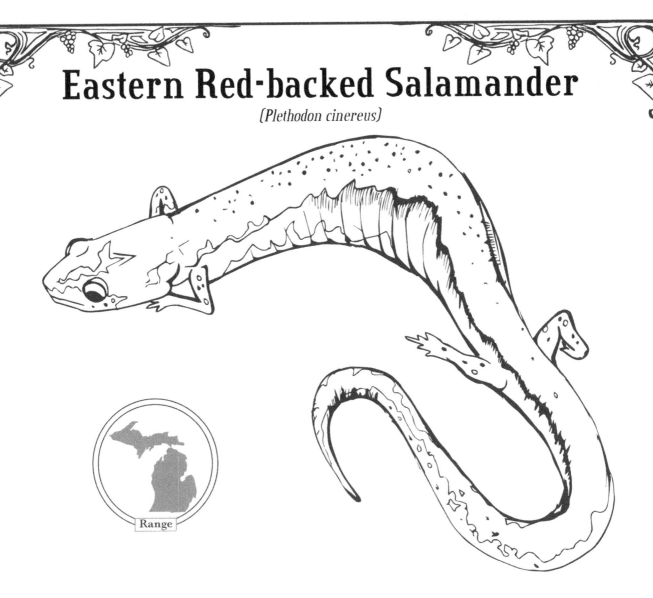

Range

ABOUT: Red-backed salamanders are very common in Michigan. They have two color phases, either "red-back" (dark with a red stripe) or "lead-back" (dark with white spots). They have long, thin bodies and tiny legs with four toes on their front feet, and five on their back feet. They don't make noise, but do communicate with each other by leaving scent trails to mark their territories.

SIZE: Length: 2 to 5 in.

DIET: Red-backed salamanders eat small invertebrates such as worms, spiders, and ants. They can survive off food stored in their bodies when the weather is too hot or too cold.

HABITAT: These terrestrial salamanders live in the cool, damp leaf-litter of forest floors. Look for them under logs and rocks, and on rainy nights.

LIFE CYCLE

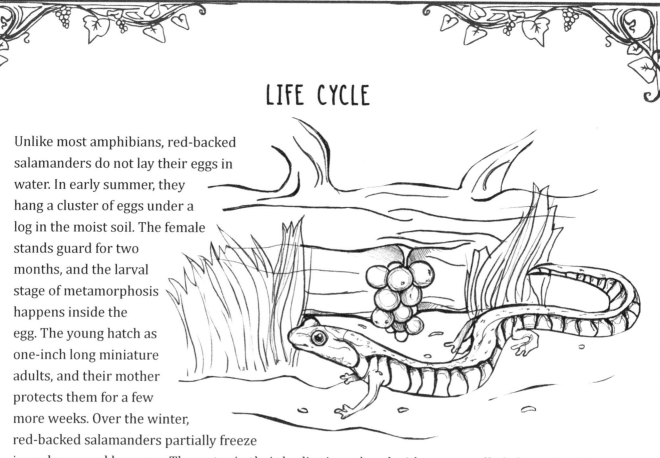

Unlike most amphibians, red-backed salamanders do not lay their eggs in water. In early summer, they hang a cluster of eggs under a log in the moist soil. The female stands guard for two months, and the larval stage of metamorphosis happens inside the egg. The young hatch as one-inch long miniature adults, and their mother protects them for a few more weeks. Over the winter, red-backed salamanders partially freeze in underground burrows. The water in their bodies is replaced with a sugar called glycerol so that internal ice crystals can't form. Their lifespan is 5 to 15 years.

NATURE KNOWLEDGE

• Since red-backed salamanders breathe through their skin and never develop lungs, they must always stay moist.

• They can drop their tails to escape predators, and it regrows a lighter color.

• When red-backed salamanders tunnel through the soil, they help to mix up nutrients which improves the soil quality for plants and invertebrates.

• They are a keystone species in their habitat, and a symbol of a healthy environment.

Gray Tree Frog
(Hyla versicolor)

Range

ABOUT: Gray tree frogs change the color of their skin depending on their environment. They can be brown, gray, or bright green with dark blotches. They have moist bumpy skin, a dark stripe behind their eyes, and bright yellow patches under their back legs. Large sticky circles on the tips of their toes help them to climb up trees and walls. The male gray tree frog has a dark chin, and his call is a short musical chirp that repeats every few seconds.

SIZE: Length: 1.25 to 2.5 in. (females are larger)

DIET: Adults eat thousands of insects and spiders a year. Tadpoles are plant eaters.

HABITAT: Gray tree frogs are arboreal and nocturnal. They live high in the treetops of forests, swamps, and backyards. They can be found on windows and walls near outdoor lights.

LIFE CYCLE

Each year in May, male gray tree frogs call from leaves that overhang water. Females lay small clusters of 30 to 40 eggs that hatch in 3-6 days. The greenish colored tadpoles go through metamorphosis by late summer. In wintertime, they hibernate under logs, rocks, roots, and leaf litter. Their bodies partially freeze and a sugar called glycerol acts as an "antifreeze" to keep internal ice crystals from forming. Their lifespan is 7 to 9 years.

NATURE KNOWLEDGE

- The Cope's gray tree frog looks almost exactly like the gray tree frog, but it has smoother skin and a faster trilling call.

- Frog fossil evidence dates back over 200 million years, from even before the dinosaurs.

- Frogs use their long tongues to catch their prey. Their large eyeballs help them to swallow by sinking into their mouth and mashing up their food.

When male frogs call, their throat pouch blows up like a bubble.

Mudpuppy
(Necturus maculosus)

Range

ABOUT: Mudpuppies are large, permanently aquatic salamanders that are also known as waterdogs. They have long brown or gray bodies, flat heads, and tiny legs with four toes on their feet. They breathe through both their slimy skin, and red leafy-looking gills that are behind their head. Mudpuppies make a squeaking sound that sounds like a dog's bark.

SIZE: Length: 8 to17 in.

DIET: Mudpuppies are carnivores that eat small fish, worms, snails, crayfish, insect larvae, frogs, and tadpoles.

HABITAT: Mudpuppies crawl along the bottoms of permanent bodies of water.

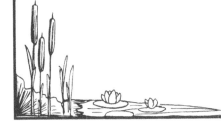

LIFE CYCLE

Female mudpuppies reach their breeding age after six years. They build a nest in the spring underneath a rock or a log and stay to guard their 30 to 150 eggs for a few months. Mudpuppies are active year-round and move slowly in the winter underneath the ice in lakes. Their lifespan is 10-20 years.

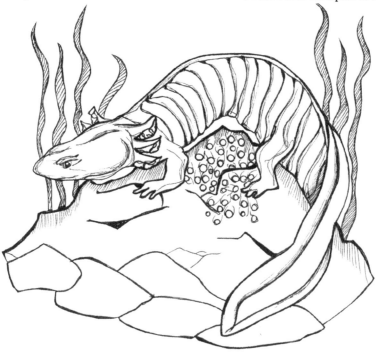

NATURE KNOWLEDGE

- The largest mudpuppy ever recorded in Michigan was 19.13 inches long. The deepest a mudpuppy has ever been found is 90 feet!

- Mudpuppies are not harmful to humans, and there is no evidence that they cause damage to fish populations.

- They are protected as a Species of Special Concern in Michigan, and are sensitive to pollution.

- The western lesser siren is another kind of large aquatic salamander, but it is extremely rare. Sirens have two tiny front legs and an eel-like body.

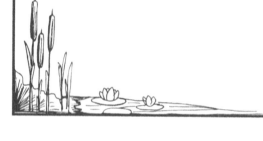

Wood Frog

(Rana sylvatica)

Range

ABOUT: Wood frogs can live farther north than any other North American amphibian. They are usually brown, with a dark "mask" across their eye, and a white stripe along their lip. When males gather at breeding ponds, their calls sound like quacking ducks.

SIZE: Length: 1 to 3.25 in. (females are larger)

DIET: Adults eat invertebrates such as flies, mosquitos, slugs, beetles, and crickets. Tadpoles mostly eat aquatic plants.

HABITAT: They are terrestrial, and are found in forested areas near water.

LIFE CYCLE

In early spring, female wood frogs lay clusters of up to 3,000 eggs in ponds. Large brown tadpoles hatch a few weeks later, and transform within a few months. In winter, wood frogs are frozen alive in the moist leaf-litter. Their blood stops flowing, and their breathing and heart rate stops. Their body produces high amounts of internal glucose, which keeps their cells from freezing. Their lifespan is 3 to 5 years.

Leaf litter is important habitat for many creatures.

NATURE KNOWLEDGE

• The amount of time that it takes frog eggs to hatch, and tadpoles to transform, depends on the surrounding temperature. In warm water, tadpoles might hatch in four days, and in colder water, it could take up to four weeks. Complete metamorphosis occurs over six to fifteen weeks.

• In the spring, large groups of wood frogs travel together to their breeding ponds, and sometimes cross roads.

• It only takes wood frogs one day of warm spring weather to unfreeze. They become active a month earlier than other frogs, and will even breed in puddles of melting snow.

Amphibian Activities
MAKE ART: Wheel of Metamorphosis

- Make a wheel of metamorphosis by drawing the life cycle of a frog around the edge of a paper plate.
- Cut a wedge out of another paper plate and attach them with a brad to make your wheel turn.

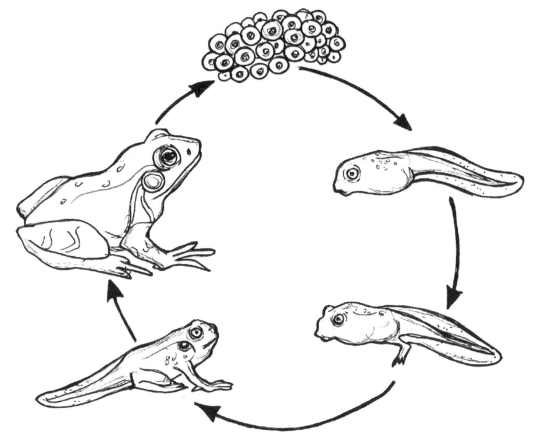

EXPERIMENT WITH SCIENCE: Amphibian Slime

- Many amphibians have a coat of slime that protects their skin from bacteria, pollution, and damage. Make your own amphibian slime with water, food coloring, and cornstarch.
- Pour one cup of corn starch into a bowl and add a quarter cup of water.
- Mix them together with your fingers until your slime feels thick like honey. Keep adding a little bit of corn starch and a little bit of water until it is the right consistency. If you poke your finger at the top of the bowl quickly, the surface will feel hard, but if you let your finger slowly sink, it will feel like a liquid.
- When your mixture is right, add two drops of food coloring. Play around with it by squeezing it into a hard ball, and then letting it slime down your fingers!

PLAY GAMES: Human Frog Chorus

- Frogs call when they are scared, trying to attract a mate, or protecting their territory. Different species make different calls, and you can learn how to identify frogs by the sound they make, just like birds. Practice frog calls with a group of friends to make a human frog chorus.
- Many arboreal frogs sing by filling up air sacs at their throats. Practice making the sound of a tree frog by pinching your nose and using a nasally voice to say: "hey ba-by, hey ba-by, hey ba-by."
- Terrestrial frogs often have low, deep voices. Pretend to be a pickerel frog by pinching your nose and sounding like a sheep: "maaaaa maaaaaaaaaaaaa maaaaa."
- Aquatic frogs make loud sounds that carry long distances. To sound like an American bullfrog, use a deep voice to say: "rum, rum, jug-o-rum, rum; rum, rum, jug-o-rum, rum."

EXPLORE NATURE: Look & Learn

Amphibians are all around us! In the spring, look for tadpoles and frog eggs in ponds. When American toads complete their metamorphosis in early summer, there can suddenly be hundreds of tiny toads hopping around in yards and forests.

Find red-backed salamanders under logs near rivers and lakes, and tree frogs on the sides of your house at night. Look for mole salamanders on rainy summer nights, or during their annual migration to breeding ponds in very early spring.

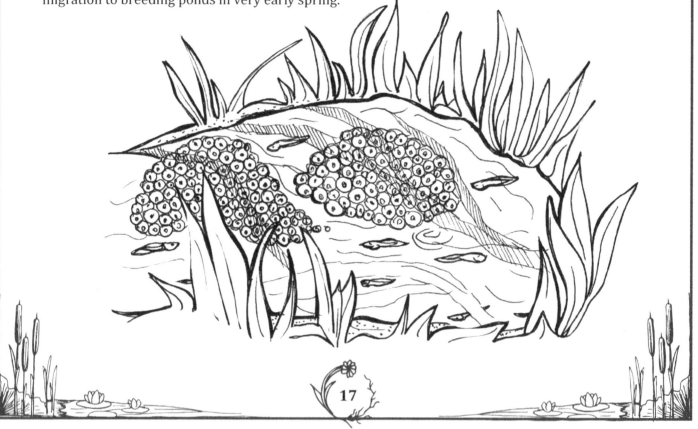

REPTILES

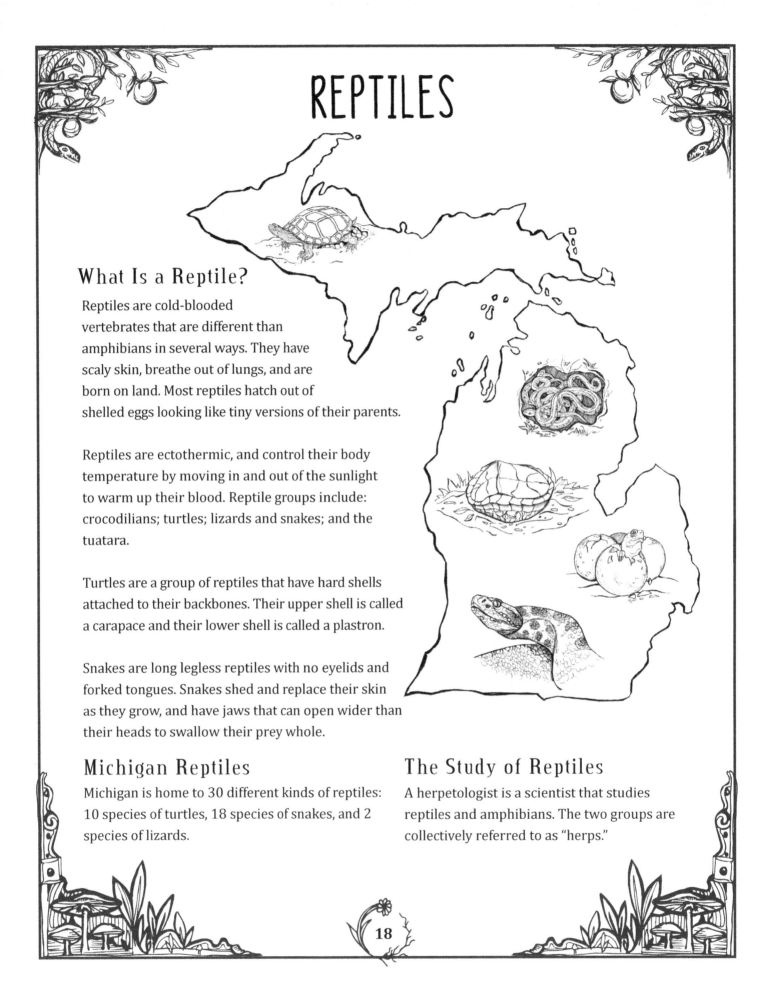

What Is a Reptile?

Reptiles are cold-blooded vertebrates that are different than amphibians in several ways. They have scaly skin, breathe out of lungs, and are born on land. Most reptiles hatch out of shelled eggs looking like tiny versions of their parents.

Reptiles are ectothermic, and control their body temperature by moving in and out of the sunlight to warm up their blood. Reptile groups include: crocodilians; turtles; lizards and snakes; and the tuatara.

Turtles are a group of reptiles that have hard shells attached to their backbones. Their upper shell is called a carapace and their lower shell is called a plastron.

Snakes are long legless reptiles with no eyelids and forked tongues. Snakes shed and replace their skin as they grow, and have jaws that can open wider than their heads to swallow their prey whole.

Michigan Reptiles

Michigan is home to 30 different kinds of reptiles: 10 species of turtles, 18 species of snakes, and 2 species of lizards.

The Study of Reptiles

A herpetologist is a scientist that studies reptiles and amphibians. The two groups are collectively referred to as "herps."

Reptile Encounters

Watch out for turtles on the road during their nesting season in May and June. Mother turtles travel from their normal habitats to find a dry place to lay their eggs.

Always help a turtle to cross the road in the same direction that they were going. Be safe and aware of cars. Try to walk behind the turtle to encourage it to move instead of picking it up. Do not pick up turtles by their tails, it can damage their backbone.

Mother turtles that are on an egg laying mission act like they are in a daze. They are so calm, that people sometimes think they should take them home as pets. What they need is help crossing safely to their nesting grounds.

Look for excavated turtle nests on river banks. Raccoons love to eat turtle eggs, so you might find a nest with eggshells around it that has been dug up.

Common map turtles are found throughout much of the lower peninsula.

Common Garter Snake

(Thamnophis sirtalis)

Range

ABOUT: The most frequently seen snake in Michigan is diurnal, terrestrial, and adaptable. Garter snakes are gray, brown, black, or olive, with three light stripes running down their back. They communicate through touch and smell, and can find each other by following scented trails.

SIZE: Length: 2 to 4 ft. (females are larger)

DIET: All snakes are carnivores. Garter snakes catch their prey by a quick "grab and swallow" technique. They eat amphibians, fish, small mammals, insects, eggs, and earthworms.

HABITAT: They are found near water in backyards, fields, and forests.

LIFE CYCLE

In late summer, garter snake females have 10-40 live babies. They are about six inches long at birth and grow quickly. They usually spend the winter hibernating with other snakes under rocks, or in mammal burrows. Their lifespan is 2 to 10 years.

Garter snake winter dens may have thousands of snakes, including other species.

NATURE KNOWLEDGE

- Garter snakes are often mistakenly called "garden snakes."

- Snakes "smell" by flicking their forked tongues in and out of their mouths. They collect pheromones from the air, then touch their tongue to the roof of their mouth to send a message to their brain.

- Most reptiles lay leathery shelled eggs, but there are some snakes that are ovoviviparous such as the massasauga and the garter snake. Their eggs hatch inside their body and the babies are born alive.

- When common garter snakes are scared or picked up, they might release a musky smelling liquid.

- Garter snakes are the northernmost snake in the Americas. They are the first snakes to emerge in the spring and can travel across snow.

Eastern Box Turtle

(Terrapene carolina)

Range

ABOUT: Box turtles have a hinged shell that can close-up like a box to protect their head, tail, and legs. Their carapace is helmet shaped with yellow or orange patterns. Males have red eyes, curved claws, and a concave plastron. Females have brown eyes and a flat plastron.

SIZE: Length: 4 to 8 in.

DIET: Box turtles are omnivores that eat a wide variety of plants and animals, including: earthworms, fruit, mice, berries, snails, mushrooms, slugs, insects, and frogs.

HABITAT: Michigan's only terrestrial turtle, they occupy small home ranges in forests, meadows, dunes, and marshes.

LIFE CYCLE

Adult female box turtles dig a hole in the ground in June to bury 3 to 8 oval shaped eggs that hatch about 90 days later. They dig deep into the dirt and stay dormant for the winter, partially freezing and living off the fat stored in their body. Their lifespan is usually 30 to 50 years, but they can live to be over 100.

The hinge on a box turtle's plastron allows them to completely protect their body parts from predators.

NATURE KNOWLEDGE

- Baby turtles have many predators because their shells take a few year to harden.

- Tortoises are turtles that live on land and cannot swim. Box turtles are not considered tortoises because, although they are not aquatic, they can swim if they need to.

- Eastern box turtles are important seed dispersers for Michigan's woodlands, and protected by law as a Species of Special Concern. They are rare due to habitat loss, collection for the pet trade, and incidents with cars.

Eastern Massasauga Rattlesnake
(Sistrurus catenatus)

Range

ABOUT: The only venomous snake in Michigan is the massasauga rattler (aka swamp rattler). They are part of a group of snakes known as pit vipers that use heat sensing organs on their heads to find prey. They are gray and black, with small dark rattles that they shake when they feel threatened.

SIZE: Length: 1 to 4 ft.

DIET: Massasaugas are predators that inject venom into their prey through hollow fangs. They mostly eat mice, as well as birds, amphibians, and insects.

HABITAT: Massasaugas are terrestrial, and are found in swamps, prairie wetlands, and river valleys. Their name comes from a Chippewa word meaning: "great river mouth."

LIFE CYCLE

Adult massasauga females give birth to up to 20 live babies every summer. They are active from April to October, and winter in dens below the frost line. Their lifespan is 20 to 25 years.

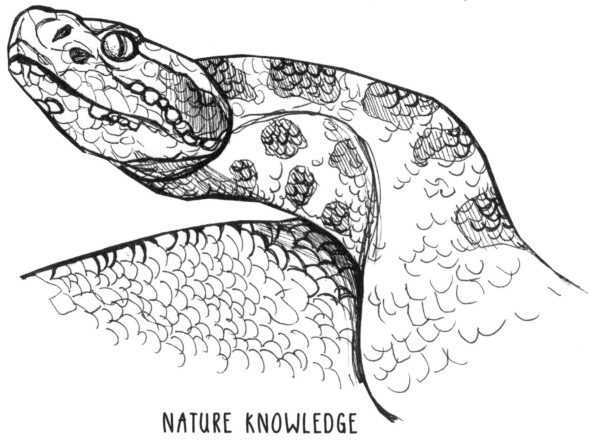

NATURE KNOWLEDGE

• Snakes are considered venomous rather than poisonous because poison is something that is swallowed, and venom is injected into the body.

• Many venomous snakes have elongated eyes with cat-like pupils and large, triangular shaped heads. Non-venomous snakes usually have round eyes and small heads.

• Massasauga's are rare, shy, and nonaggressive. They are afraid of people, and try to leave or hide when encountered. There has not been a death from a massasauga in over 100 years, and bites are easily treated at hospitals.

• Massasaugas are protected as a Threatened Species in Michigan.

Painted Turtle

(Chrysemys picta)

Range

ABOUT: Michigan's state turtle has a red patterned shell, and yellow and red stripes on their head, neck, and feet. They have adapted to live near people, and are the most common turtle in Michigan. They communicate with each other through touch. Males have long front nails.

SIZE: Length: 4 to 10 in.

DIET: Painted turtles are omnivores that eat a variety of fish, aquatic plants, seeds, crayfish, frogs, and insects.

HABITAT: They are diurnal, and can be seen basking in the sun on logs in shallow ponds, lakes, and wetlands.

LIFE CYCLE

Adult female painted turtles dig a nest each June to bury 4 to 15 eggs that hatch in about 80 days. Babies can remain in their nest until the following spring, and partially freeze for the winter. Adults hibernate on muddy river bottoms. Their lifespan is 30 to 55 years.

Female painted turtles lay 2-5 clutch's per year.

NATURE KNOWLEDGE

• Very cold tolerant, painted turtles are sometimes seen swimming under the ice in late winter.

• Red-eared sliders are a common pet turtle that looks similar, but they have a rounder carapace, a bright red mark on the side of their face, and a spotted plastron.

• If a turtle lays eggs in your yard, you can help protect the eggs from predators by staking down chicken wire over the nest that has holes wide enough for baby turtles to get through. Raccoons love to eat turtle eggs, but won't figure out how to burrow under the wire.

Snapping Turtle

(Chelydra serpentina)

Range

ABOUT: Snapping turtles are the biggest turtle in Michigan. They are brown or black with long spiky tails, a big head, webbed feet, long claws, and a ridged shell. Do not try to pick up a snapping turtle, they have large jaws and can bite hard! Snapping turtles use leg and head movements to communicate.

SIZE: Length: 1-2 feet (males are larger).

DIET: Snapping turtles are opportunistic omnivores. They eat anything that is convenient, including: plants, small mammals, crayfish, frogs, fish, leeches, and insects.

HABITAT: Snapping turtles are aquatic and mostly nocturnal. They are found in ponds, rivers, lakes, and streams.

LIFE CYCLE

In June, adult female snapping turtles lay from 10 to 100 eggs. Depending on the temperature, babies hatch between 55 to 105 days later. In the winter, snapping turtles hibernate on muddy river bottoms, underneath logs, or in muskrat burrows. Their average lifespan in the wild is around 30 years, but they have been known to live for 75 years.

NATURE KNOWLEDGE

• The temperature of the environment determines whether turtle eggs are males or females. If the temperature is above 84 degrees Fahrenheit, they will be females. If the temperature is lower, they will be males.

• Turtles have been on the earth longer than dinosaurs, and snapping turtles are some of the most ancient. They have not changed much in 40 million years.

Reptile Activities

MAKE ART: Reptile Clips

- Draw and cut out your favorite Michigan reptile on a piece of cardstock.
- Attach it to a wooden clothespin and glue a magnet to the other side.

EXPERIMENT WITH SCIENCE: Snake Science

Snakes have no legs, which makes catching their prey and shedding their skin difficult. All snakes swallow their prey whole. Their jawbones are attached loosely to the back of their skull. Stretchy ligaments allow them to open their mouth very wide. Stretch a rubber band with your fingers to see how a snake jaw opens.

Snakes have different ways of hunting:

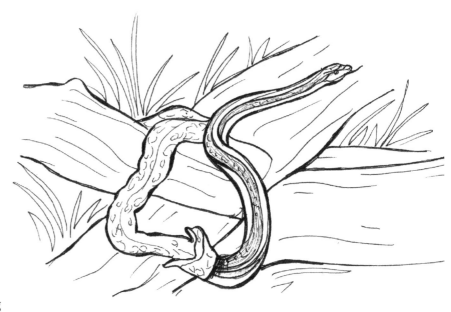

- Some grab their prey quickly like a garter snake and swallow them alive.
- Others, like the massasauga, kill their prey with venom.
- Constrictors, like the eastern fox snake, wrap around prey and squeeze it.

Practice being a snake shedding its skin by pulling a tight sock over your arm. Try to get it off without using your hands. It takes 18 to 24 hours for snakes to shed their skin. The old skin comes off in one long piece, and a new larger skin is underneath. If you find a snake skin for your nature collection, examine it. How do the scales feel different than amphibian slime? Ask at your local pet store if they will save you a snake skin for your research.

PLAY GAMES: Michigan Predator & Prey

• Many Michigan reptiles are predators. Predators eat other animals which are called prey. Choose 1 to 3 predators, depending on group size, to start out in the middle of a playing field. Decide which kind of Michigan predator they will be for each round.

• The rest of the group stands on one side of the playing field. The prey will decide on three different Michigan prey animals to choose from. (For example, if the predators are snapping turtles, the prey could choose between crayfish, tadpoles, or fish.)

• The predators decide what they are hungry for, and call out one of the options. If you decide that you are a tadpole, and the predators call out "tadpole", then you and the other "tadpoles" try to run to the other side of the playing field without getting tagged. Crayfish and fish wait until the predators call them. Prey may not switch their animal during the round.

• If you are tagged, you freeze and become a tree. Trees are rooted in the ground and can no longer run, but your arms are branches that can wave in the wind and tag other animals.

• Play continues until there are 1 to 3 players left untagged to be the next predators. New predators pick a new Michigan animal and three things that that animal eats for the next round.

EXPLORE NATURE: Turtle Tracks

• Look for turtles basking in the sun on logs during the day. Find signs of turtles in the mud near your local pond or river. Their tracks look like circles with small dots around them that might have a tail drag line. If you find pieces of turtle shells, look for small bite marks where rodents have chewed on the bony shells as a source of calcium.

• Look for northern water snakes in the long grasses near pond and river edges. Do not pick up a wild snake, even if they are not venomous, they can still bite.

BIRDS

What Is a Bird?

Birds are warm-blooded vertebrates with feathers. They lay hard-shelled eggs, and have a beak, two feet, wings, and hollow bones. Most birds build nests and sit on their eggs to incubate them. Newborn birds are called hatchlings, and while learning to fly, they are called fledglings.

Many of Michigan's birds migrate south in the fall. They fly to warmer places where it is easier to find food in the winter. Each spring, they return to Michigan to lay their eggs. They raise their young during the warm summer months when there is plenty of food.

Michigan Birds

Of the 800 species of North American birds, 450 have been recorded in Michigan.

The Study of Birds

People that like to look for and identify birds are known as birdwatchers or birders. Scientists who study birds are called ornithologists.

Bird Encounters

Observe birds through a pair of binoculars to learn more about them. Native plants and a birdfeeder in your yard will attract birds, and provide a resting spot for them as they migrate across the state.

Northern cardinals are red birds often seen in backyards.

Bird ID Guide

Identify birds with these simple steps:

- **What size and shape is the bird?**

    o Notice the shape of the bird's body and estimate its size by comparing it to a common bird. Look to see if the bird is small like a House Sparrow, medium like an American Robin, or large like an American Crow.

    o The outline of a bird against the sky is called a silhouette. Learning to recognize common silhouettes can help you with identification.

- **What does the bird's beak look like?**

    o A bird beak is also called a bill. Look at the color, shape, markings, and size of the bill to find out more about what the bird eats and where it lives.

- **What color is the bird?**

    o Observe the overall color of the bird. Note the color of the wings, breast, tail-feathers, and legs. Many guidebooks are divided by color.

- **What kind of habitat is the bird in?**

    o Notice where the bird is and how it is behaving.

- **What sounds does the bird make?**

    o Every bird makes a unique noise. It is easier to hear a bird than to see a bird. Listen to recordings to learn bird calls.

American Robin

(Turdus migratorius)

Tracks

Range

ABOUT: Michigan's state bird has a gray body with an orange breast, white eye circles, and a yellow bill. These songbirds begin whistling songs in the early morning, and are often seen hopping around in yards pulling earthworms out of the ground.

SIZE: Height: 7 to 11 in. Wingspan: 12 to 16 in.

DIET: Seasonal omnivores, they forage for insects and earthworms in the spring and summer, and for fruit, berries, and seeds in the fall and winter.

HABITAT: American Robins live in forests, farms, and neighborhoods.

LIFE CYCLE

Some robins migrate for the winter, while others stay in Michigan year-round, and roost together by the thousands for warmth. In early spring, females build a cup-shaped nest out of twigs, mud, and grass for their 3-5 blue eggs. They hatch after a couple of weeks, and leave the nest a few weeks later. They can have 2 to 3 broods per year. Their lifespan is 6 to 14 years.

NATURE KNOWLEDGE

• All birds can make a call that has a single sound, but only songbirds can produce a song that is a series of repeated musical notes.

• Songbirds are also known as perching birds. They have three toes on their feet that point forward, and one that points backward, to help them hold onto branches.

• When American Robins forage on lawns they can be poisoned by pesticides, and become indicators of a polluted area.

Bald Eagle

(Haliaeetus leucocephalus)

Range

Tracks

ABOUT: The national bird is a large raptor with a dark brown body, a white head and tail feathers, and a bright yellow bill and legs. Immature Bald Eagles are a speckled brown color. They don't get their white feathers until about four years old. Their call is shrill and high-pitched, and sounds like: "Kleek-kik-ik-ik-ik" or "kak-kak-kak."

SIZE: Height: 3 ft. Wingspan: 6 to 8 ft. (females are larger).

DIET: Eagles are carnivores and scavengers. They eat fish, small mammals, birds, and carrion.

HABITAT: Found year-round in Michigan near lakes, rivers, and coasts.

LIFE CYCLE

Bald Eagle nests are huge platforms built out of branches and mud that can be up to eight feet long. Eagles mate for life and use the same nest each year. Females lay 1 to 3 large white eggs, and both parents help to incubate them for about a month. Chicks leave the nest after three months and stay nearby as they learn to fly. Immature eagles are nomadic and solitary and can travel hundreds of miles a day. They choose a mate around the age of five. Their lifespan is 20 to 36 years.

Juvenile Bald Eagles are all dark brown and are the same size as their parents.

NATURE KNOWLEDGE

• Once rare in Michigan, Bald Eagles are an example of an endangered species success story. After protecting nesting habitat and banning the use of the pesticide DDT, they are now common.

• Bald Eagles will steal fish from Ospreys, because Ospreys have sandpaper like coated talons that make it easier to grab slippery fish out of the water.

• When Bald Eagles soar, their wings are perfectly straight, unlike the upwards "V" silhouette of a Turkey Vulture's wings.

Barred Owl

(Strix varia)

Range

Tracks

ABOUT: Barred Owls are large, nocturnal raptors with white and brown stripes, a yellow bill, and a white face with dark eye rings. They are very vocal, and have many different calls. Their most common call sounds like: "who cooks for you, who cooks for you-all?"

SIZE: Height: 16 to 25 in. Wingspan: 3 to 4 ft.

DIET: These opportunistic predators hunt for small rodents, insects, reptiles, and birds. They wade in water to catch frogs, crayfish, turtles, and fish.

HABITAT: Barred Owls are found in mature mixed forests near the water.

Barred Owls search for aquatic prey in shallow water.

LIFE CYCLE

Barred Owls build nests 20 to 40 feet high in tree cavities, old squirrels' nests, or abandoned platform nests. They lay 1 to 5 white eggs each spring that are incubated for about a month. Chicks begin to leave the nest after another month. Barred Owls are seen year-round in Michigan. Their lifespan is 10 to 23 years.

NATURE KNOWLEDGE

• Owls have flat faces and their eyes look straight ahead. They can turn their heads 270 degrees in each direction to see to their sides.

• All raptors, including owls have specially modified feathers. Serrated edges allow them to fly silently by breaking up the turbulence of air-flow over the feathers. A soft downy edge lessens noise from feathers rubbing against each other.

• After eating, owls leave behind a pellet that looks like scat, but is actually undigested bones, fur, and feathers.

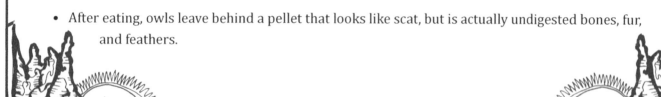

Black-capped Chickadee

(Poecile atricapillus)

Range

Tracks

ABOUT: Black-capped Chickadees are small curious birds that are often seen near homes. They are tan with gray wings, a white breast and cheeks, and a black head and neck. Chickadees are named after their most common call: "chick-a-dee-dee-dee."

SIZE: Height: 5 in. Wingspan: 6 to 8 in.

DIET: Chickadees are omnivores that eat seeds, berries, and insects.

HABITAT: They are found in forests and around human development.

LIFE CYCLE

Black-capped Chickadees are cavity nesters that lay 5 to 7 white eggs with brown speckles each spring. The female incubates the eggs for two weeks while her mate brings her food. They stay together as a family group for about six weeks. They are year-round residents of Michigan. Their lifespan is typically 2 to 3 years.

Chickadees are seed dispersers.

NATURE KNOWLEDGE

• Other bird species respond to Black-capped Chickadee alarm calls. More "dee" sounds at the end of a call announces a bigger threat.

• Active even in the worst winter weather, chickadees must eat every day. Their good memories help them find food that they stored in thousands of different places.

• Chickadees go into a state of torpor to conserve energy. They survive cold winter nights by lowering their body temperature about 20 degrees Fahrenheit.

Canada Goose

(Branta canadensis)

Range

Tracks

ABOUT: Canada Geese are large brown birds with a black and white head, and a long black neck. They migrate in "V" shaped formations that help them to be more aerodynamic. Traveling over 1,500 miles in 24 hours, they honk along the way and stop at routine resting areas. Males nod their heads and hiss to protect their territory.

SIZE: Height: 2 to 3.5 ft. Wingspan: 4 to 6 ft.

DIET: Herbivores, they graze on land for grasses, grains, and berries, and forage for aquatic plants in the water.

HABITAT: Canada Geese are found near water in fields, parks, and farms.

LIFE CYCLE

Canada Geese make large cup-shaped ground nests that are lined with grass and moss for their 5 to 10 white eggs. Females sit on their nest for almost a month, while their mate stays nearby as a guard. Downy yellow hatchlings can leave the nest and swim when they are only a few days old. These natural migrators travel throughout the U.S.A. and Canada, and can live up to 30 years old.

NATURE KNOWLEDGE

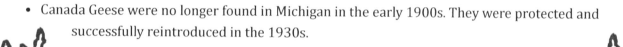

- Adults molt their flight feathers while they are raising their young, and their whole family is flightless for part of the summer.

- The correct way to refer to a group of this bird is "Canada geese," although many people will say "Canadian Geese."

- Canada Geese were no longer found in Michigan in the early 1900s. They were protected and successfully reintroduced in the 1930s.

Pileated Woodpecker

(Dryocopus pileatus)

Tracks

Range

ABOUT: Pileated Woodpeckers are the largest woodpeckers in Michigan. They have black backs, a bright red crest on their heads, a red mustache, and yellow eyes. Males have red foreheads, and females have grey-brown foreheads. They use their strong pointed bills to peck holes in trees which makes a drumming sound that can be heard across long distances. Their alarm call is a short "wuk, wuk" sound.

SIZE: Height: 19 in. Wingspan: 26 to 30 in.

DIET: Omnivores, they eat carpenter ants, beetles, caterpillars, insect larva, fruit, and nuts.

HABITAT: Woodpeckers are found in coniferous, deciduous, and mixed forests.

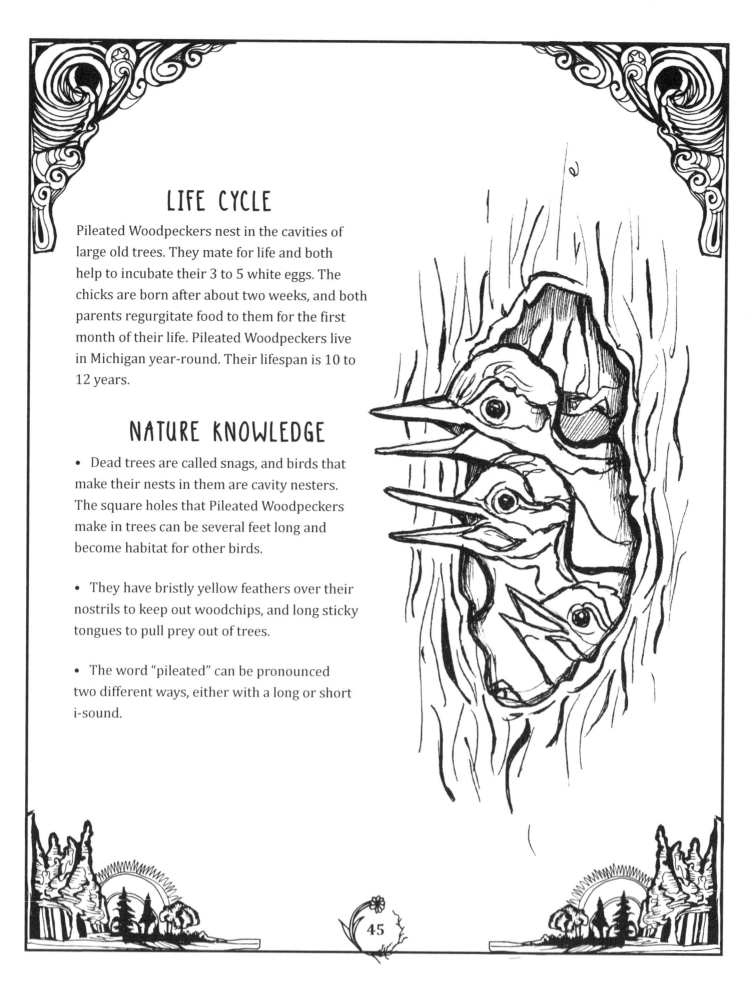

LIFE CYCLE

Pileated Woodpeckers nest in the cavities of large old trees. They mate for life and both help to incubate their 3 to 5 white eggs. The chicks are born after about two weeks, and both parents regurgitate food to them for the first month of their life. Pileated Woodpeckers live in Michigan year-round. Their lifespan is 10 to 12 years.

NATURE KNOWLEDGE

• Dead trees are called snags, and birds that make their nests in them are cavity nesters. The square holes that Pileated Woodpeckers make in trees can be several feet long and become habitat for other birds.

• They have bristly yellow feathers over their nostrils to keep out woodchips, and long sticky tongues to pull prey out of trees.

• The word "pileated" can be pronounced two different ways, either with a long or short i-sound.

Red-tailed Hawk

(Buteo jamaicensis)

Tracks

Range

ABOUT: Red-tailed Hawks are Michigan's most common raptor. They are brown and white with red tail-feathers, and a dark spot near their shoulders. Juveniles do not have a red tail. Their call is a screaming "ke-eeee-ar" sound that lasts about two seconds.

SIZE: Height: 19-25 in. Wingspan: 4.5 ft.

DIET: Carnivores, they eat small reptiles, mammals, and birds.

HABITAT: They live in fields and forests along the edges of roads, and perch on light posts and telephone poles.

LIFE CYCLE

Red-tailed Hawks mate for life. They return each year to a platform nest made with large sticks and lined with pine needles. Females lay 2 to 3 white eggs. Mates take turns incubating the eggs for a month, and feeding their young together for about a month. They are partial migrators. Their lifespan is 10 to 25 years.

Red-tailed hawk's favorite food is small mammals.

NATURE KNOWLEDGE

• Raptors are birds that catch their food with their feet instead of their beaks. Their strong feet with sharp claws are called talons. They tear apart their food with sharp curved beaks, have excellent eyesight, and specially modified feathers. Hawks, owls, eagles, kites, falcons, and kestrels are raptors.

• Partial migrators do not follow a regular migration pattern of going to the same place at the same time every year. They wait until food is hard to find and fly as far south as they can find food. Some years, they might not leave, and in other years, they might fly hundreds or thousands of miles.

Ring-billed Gull

(Larus delawarensis)

Tracks

Range

ABOUT: Ring-billed Gulls have adapted to scavenge for food in cities. They are white with gray wings and yellow feet. You can tell them apart from other gulls by the black ring on the tip of their beak. Their common alarm call is a high-pitched "kree, kree" sound.

SIZE: Height: 18 to 20 in. Wingspan: 3 ft.

DIET: These opportunistic omnivores will eat anything that they can find. This includes fish, insects, rodents, eggs, fruit, aquatic animals, grain, seeds, garbage, and human food.

HABITAT: Ring-billed Gulls are found near lakes, dunes, garbage dumps, beaches, parking lots, and neighborhoods.

LIFE CYCLE

Ring-billed Gulls usually nest in large colonies on the beach. Mated pairs take turns sitting on their 2 to 4 blue and brown spotted eggs for about a month. Chicks can leave the nest within a few days, and fly a month later. Some are complete migrators, and others stay year-round. Their lifespan is 3 to 23 years.

NATURE KNOWLEDGE

• Aquatic birds are also called waterfowl. They have webbed feet to help them to dive and swim.

• Ring-billed Gulls are good at stealing food from people and other birds. They practice by playing games in their colonies, where they drop an object and swoop down to get it.

• Ring-billed Gull hatchlings can be gray or pink with white spots. First-year birds are white with brown flecks and a dark tail. The ring on their beak appears after their first winter. Second-year birds are mostly gray with a dark band at the end of their tail. Their adult plumage grows in when they reach maturity at about three years old.

Ruffed Grouse

(Bonasa umbellus)

Tracks

Range

ABOUT: Ruffed Grouse are medium-sized ground birds that are either gray or reddish brown. They have a long square tail and a crest of feathers on their head. They are usually very quiet but can make hissing, cooing, and whining sounds.

SIZE: Height: 16 to 19 in. Wingspan: 20 to 25 in.

DIET: Omnivores, they forage for food on the ground such as fruit, seeds, tree buds, leaves, acorns, and insects.

HABITAT: Ruffed Grouse live in the understory of both mixed and deciduous forests. They prefer large areas of undisturbed woodlands.

LIFE CYCLE

In the spring, males perform a courtship dance with their tail-feathers fanned and the crest on their head raised. They cup their wings and beat them on logs, creating a drumming sound that can be heard for a quarter of a mile. Females scrape together leaves on the ground where they lay about a dozen tan eggs. Chicks hatch in 23 days ready to feed themselves, and begin flying in five days. They stay with their mother for over four months. They are year-round Michigan residents. Their lifespan is 3-11 years.

NATURE KNOWLEDGE

• Female Ruffed Grouse will pretend that they have broken their wing to distract predators from their chicks.

• When young males are about five months old, they choose a drumming log within a few miles of their mother. They spend the rest of their lives near that log.

• Grouse adapt to Michigan's heavy snows each year by growing extensions on their feet that act like their very own snowshoes.

Turkey Vulture

(Cathartes aura)

Tracks

Range

ABOUT: Turkey Vultures have small heads covered with wrinkly red skin instead of feathers. When they soar, their silhouette is a shallow "V" shape. Turkey Vulture wings have black and gray edges and long, finger-like tips. They make grunts and groans.

SIZE: Height: 26 to 32 in. Wingspan: 6 ft.

DIET: These scavengers eat freshly dead animals.

HABITAT: Turkey Vultures are found in all habitats throughout Michigan, and are often seen eating roadkill.

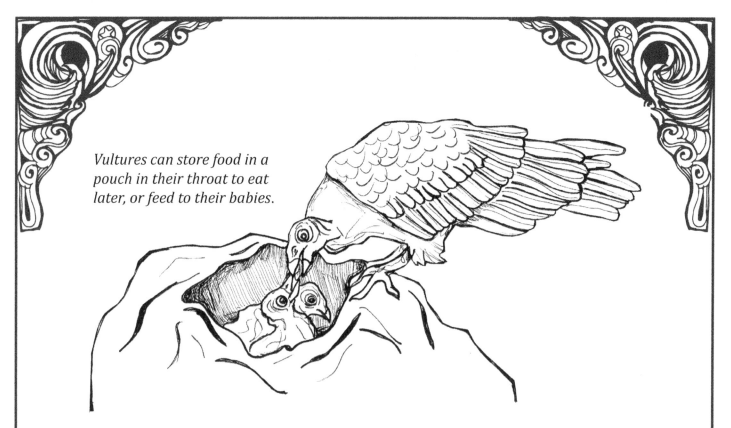

Vultures can store food in a pouch in their throat to eat later, or feed to their babies.

LIFE CYCLE

Turkey Vultures don't usually build their own nests, they use abandoned nests, mammal burrows, or hollow logs. Their two eggs are white with brown markings. Females and males both help to incubate the eggs for over a month, and then feed the young regurgitated food for another few months. They are complete migrators and can fly up to 200 miles per day. Their lifespan is 20 to 24 years.

NATURE KNOWLEDGE

- Vultures have a much better sense of smell than most birds, and excellent eyesight.

- Turkey Vultures are smaller than Bald Eagles, and larger than Red-tailed Hawks.

- Black Vultures look a lot like Turkey Vultures, but they have black heads, short tails, and a white patch on their wings.

Wild Turkey

(Meleagris gallopavo)

Tracks

Range

ABOUT: Wild Turkeys have large dark bodies with orange legs, blue heads, and red throats. They are fast runners with excellent eyesight and hearing. Males have a big fan of tail-feathers that they display during mating season. Turkeys make a variety of cackling and gobbling sounds.

SIZE: Height: 4 ft. Wingspan: 5 to 6 ft.

DIET: Omnivores, they forage on the forest floor for invertebrates, acorns, amphibians, snails, flower buds, seeds, small snakes, and berries.

HABITAT: Family flocks travel through forests, fields, and meadows.

LIFE CYCLE

Female Wild Turkeys lay 10 to 12 eggs in ground nests near forest clearings. Chicks are born in early summer and can find their own food after only a few days. They stay with their mother and join other broods to form flocks that can be as large as 200 turkeys in the winter. They are non-migrators that are active year-round. Their lifespan is 3 to 4 years.

NATURE KNOWLEDGE

• Benjamin Franklin wanted the Wild Turkey to be the national bird instead of the Bald Eagle.

• Male Wild Turkeys are called toms or gobblers, and females are called hens. Toms are almost twice as big as hens with waddles on their throats, large fantails, and sharp spurs on the backs of their legs. Their leg spurs can be over two inches long, and are used to fight other males.

• Wild Turkeys can swim by spreading their tail-feathers, kicking their strong legs, and holding their large wings close to their bodies.

• Once gone from the wild in Michigan, they have fully recovered since their reintroduction in the 1950s.

Bird Activities

MAKE ART: Recycled Binoculars

- Save two toilet-paper tubes and decorate them with paint or stickers.
- Wrap tape around them or staple them together.
- Punch a hole in each side and tie a piece of yarn that is long enough to fit over your head.
- Use your binoculars on nature walks to help you focus in on details.

PLAY GAMES: Bird Beak Buffet

Birds have different shaped beaks depending on what they eat and where they live. Most birds find and eat their food with their beaks. The only birds that catch their food with their feet are raptors.

You can practice eating like a bird by setting up a bird beak buffet. Different stations represent different ways that birds eat. Observe how the birds in your yard are using their beaks and think of your own stations, or use the following examples.

o **Ruby-throated Hummingbirds** have long thin beaks and tongues to drink nectar out of the center of flowers. Use an eye dropper to transfer colored water from one cup to another.

o **Northern Cardinals** have short beaks for cracking open seeds. Use a nutcracker to open sunflower seeds and nuts.

o **Barn Swallows** have wide beaks to catch insects in the air. Tape a cup sideways onto a table and try to throw dried beans into it.

o **American Robins** have sharp strong beaks for pulling worms out of the soil. Bury gummy worms in a bowl of dirt and use chopsticks to pick them up.

o **Mallard Ducks** strain food out of the water with spoon-like beaks. Float pieces of Styrofoam, or wooden beads, in a bowl of water and scoop them out with a slotted spoon.

o **House Finches** have short strong beaks for eating grains, seeds, and berries. Use a clothespin to try to pick up rice and dried beans.

EXPERIMENT WITH SCIENCE: Dissect an Owl Pellet

After raptors eat, they regurgitate a pellet that looks like scat. It is the undigested bones, fur, and feathers of their prey. If you find a pellet in the woods, use gloves and tweezers to dissect it and find the tiny bones of rodents and birds inside.

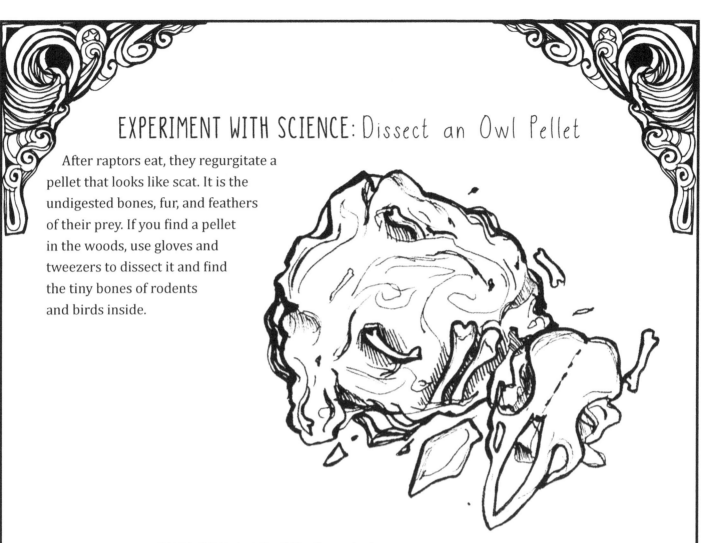

EXPLORE NATURE: Bird List

- Become a birder by making a species list of the birds that you see. Note how many there are, the date, location, and habitat. Contribute to bird data in your area by getting involved in the Great Back-yard Bird Count and the Christmas Bird Count.
- Play Bird Behavior Bingo by making a list of common bird behaviors and turning it into a bingo card.
- Make a Migration Mobile.
  - o Draw the brids that you see or copy the ones from this book.
  - o Find out which birds stay in Michigan for the winter. Investigate where the birds that migrate will go.
  - o Use yarn to hang drawings of the birds that migrate from a stick.
  - o Glue pictures of the birds that are permanent Michigan residents to the stick.
  - o Attach yarn as a hanger and hang up your mobile to remind you about Michigan migratory birds.

MAMMALS

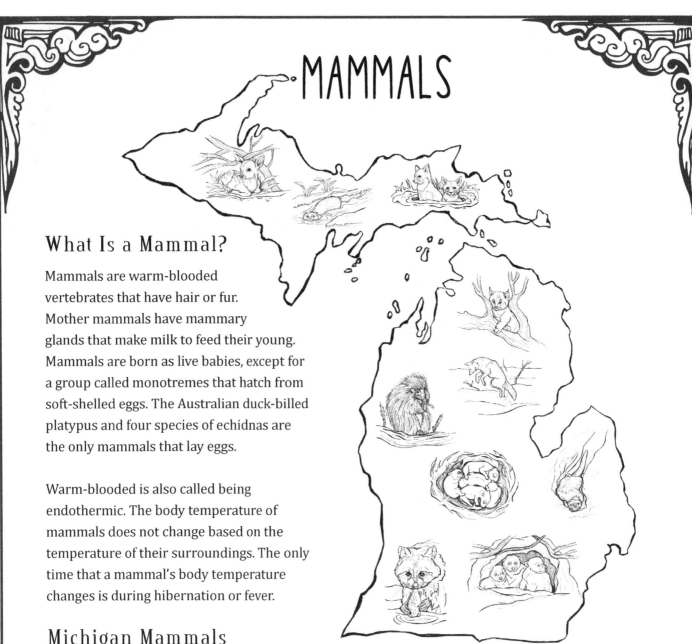

What Is a Mammal?

Mammals are warm-blooded vertebrates that have hair or fur. Mother mammals have mammary glands that make milk to feed their young. Mammals are born as live babies, except for a group called monotremes that hatch from soft-shelled eggs. The Australian duck-billed platypus and four species of echidnas are the only mammals that lay eggs.

Warm-blooded is also called being endothermic. The body temperature of mammals does not change based on the temperature of their surroundings. The only time that a mammal's body temperature changes is during hibernation or fever.

Michigan Mammals

Michigan is home to 66 species of mammals.

The Study of Mammals

The scientific study of mammals is a branch of biology called mammalogy. A naturalist studies plants and animals in their surroundings. Scatology is the biological study of animal excrement, or scat.

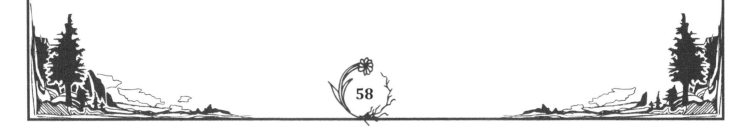

Scat, Tracks, and Signs

Wild mammals are often secretive, and the evidence that they leave behind helps naturalists to study them. The most obvious signs of mammals are scat (poop) and tracks (footprints). By learning to identify mammal signs, you can learn many things about animals, without ever actually seeing them.

When you find mammal scat, you can figure out what animal it is from by observing its size and shape. Look around for nearby clues, such as tracks and habitat. You can learn about their diet, their movements, how many of them there are, and how healthy they are. Never touch scat with your bare hands.

Wet mud and sand are good places to find mammal tracks. Look to see how big the tracks are, and count how many toes there are. Use the pictures and measurements of tracks provided in this book to help guide you.

Other signs that mammals live in an area include burrow entrances, scratches on trees, broken branches, teeth marks, packed-down grass, drag marks, nut shells, scattered seeds, and so on.

Mammal Encounters

Investigating the signs of mammals is like putting together a natural puzzle to solve a mystery. Useful tools to have with you are: a ruler, a magnifying glass, gloves, and a stick. Become a nature detective in your own backyard and attract mammals by planting native plants for them to eat, or hide in.

American Mink
(Neovison vison)

Range

Tracks

ABOUT: American minks are mustelids with long bodies, short legs, and small round ears. They have fluffy tails, dark brown fur, and a white patch on their chin. They can run quickly on land, are excellent swimmers, and are active both day and night. Communication is through chatters, snarls, and hisses.

SIZE: Length: 14 to 20 in. Tail: 6 to 8 in. Height: 8 in. Weight: 2 to 3.5 lbs. (males are larger)

DIET: Mink are opportunistic carnivores that eat rabbits, muskrats, birds, frogs, fish, crayfish, worms, chipmunks, and snakes.

SCAT: Length: 2.5 to 3 in. Diameter: 0.5 in. Mink scat is small and dark with a bad smell. It contains bones and fur, and is found on rocks or logs near the water.

TRACKS & SIGNS: Front feet: 1.5 in. Hind feet: 2.5 in. Their feet have some webbing and semi-retractable claws, and their five toed tracks look like little stars. Look for mink tracks on frozen lakes in the winter.

HABITAT: Minks are solitary and live in burrows near rivers, lakes, and ponds.

Minks have webbed feet that help them to swim up to 100 feet underwater.

LIFE CYCLE

Mink kits are born in late spring in litter sizes of 1 to 8. In less than a month, they open their eyes, and they are weaned after another month. Young stay with their mother until fall, and then leave to find their own territories. They are active year-round and hunt under the ice in the winter. Their lifespan is 5 to 10 years.

NATURE KNOWLEDGE

- To keep up with a high metabolism, American minks eat about a third of their body weight each day.

- Their fur is thick and water-resistant to keep them warm in freezing water. Mink have been hunted and trapped for their valuable fur for hundreds of years. It takes about 70 mink pelts to make one women's coat.

- The mustelid family includes: otters, wolverines, badgers, weasels, martens, ferrets, and minks. Mustelids have glands that produce a smelly oil that is used to mark their territory.

Black Bear

(Ursus americanus)

Tracks

Range

ABOUT: Black bears are the only kind of bears that live in Michigan. Their fur is usually black with a light brown snout, but they can also be all brown. Young bears often have a white patch on their chest. Black bears have good eyesight and hearing, and are excellent swimmers and climbers. Black bears grunt, groan, snort, and growl.

SIZE: Length: 4 to 7 ft. Tail: 3 to 7 in. Height: 3 to 5 ft. Weight: 90 to 500 lbs. (males are larger)

DIET: Black bears are omnivores that eat 90% plants. In the spring, they forage for green leaves and in the summer, fresh berries and insects. In the fall, they fill up with acorns and fish. Black bears can learn to eat "people food," and to open lids and latches. Do not feed bears!

SCAT: Length: 5 to 12 in. Diameter: 1.5 in. Black bear scat varies depending on what a bear has eaten. It is often large and tubular, but can be runny or full of seeds.

TRACKS & SIGNS: Front foot: 5 x 5 in. Hind Foot: 7 x 5 in. Black bear tracks have five toes with claws on each big round foot. Look for scratches on trees that have been made by teeth or claws to communicate with other bears.

HABITAT: Black bears prefer large forests with swamps and meadows. They make dens in river banks or hollow trees.

LIFE CYCLE

Black bears in Michigan usually enter their dens in December, and have 2 to 5 cubs in January. They sleep heavily for the winter and their heart rate, breathing rate, and body temperature stay very low. They do not eat or drink and live off the fat that is stored in their body. Cubs are weaned in 6 to 8 months, but they stay with their mother for about a year and a half. Black bears typically give birth every other year and their lifespan is 20-30 years.

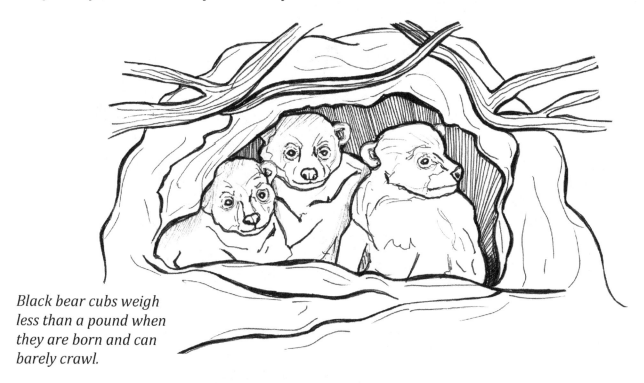

Black bear cubs weigh less than a pound when they are born and can barely crawl.

NATURE KNOWLEDGE

• Male black bears have a much larger home range (335 square miles) than females (50 square miles).

• If there are wild bears in your neighborhood, lock any trash or pet food that is kept outside in a bear-safe container.

• Black bears are not usually dangerous to people. Mothers that feel like their cubs are in trouble, or bears that are addicted to people food can be aggressive. If you see a black bear, stay calm and slowly back away. The bear will probably run away from you. If not, try to scare the bear away. Wave something around above your head, yell, and bang sticks together to make yourself as tall and loud as possible. Please note that this only works for black bears, not grizzly bears.

Bobcat

(Lynx rufus)

Range

Tracks

ABOUT: Bobcats are brown in the summer and gray in the winter. They have fuzzy ear tufts, short tails, and fur that is streaked with black spots. They are mostly nocturnal, terrestrial, and solitary. Bobcats have excellent senses of vision, hearing, and smelling, and are good climbers and swimmers. They communicate using meows, yelps, and purrs.

SIZE: Length: 2.5 to 3.5 ft. Tail: 3 to 7 in. Height: 2 ft. Weight: 14 to 30 lbs.

DIET: Carnivores that prefer to hunt for rabbits and rodents, bobcats will also eat birds, bats, snakes, small deer, and chickens.

SCAT: Length: 4 in. Diameter: 0.75 in. Scat is segmented and covered in dirt or leaves with scrape marks next to it.

TRACKS & SIGNS: Front & hind feet: 1.5 x 1.4 in. The difference between a bobcat and a coyote track is found in the claw marks. Felines retract their claws while walking; canines do not. Bobcat tracks have no claw marks, two lobes on their front heel pad, and three lobes on their rear. Bobcats mark territory with scat, scent markings, tree scratches, and piles of dirt and leaves.

HABITAT: Bobcats live in forests, dunes, swamps, and farmlands. Their dens are in hollow trees or underneath rocks, with one main den and several other smaller dens throughout their home-range.

Bobcat kittens can climb trees by the time they are a month old.

LIFE CYCLE

Bobcats have 1 to 6 kittens each spring that open their eyes after 10 days and are weaned at 12 weeks. They stay with their mother until they are about 8 to 11 months old. Bobcats are active year round. Their lifespan is 6 to 12 years.

NATURE KNOWLEDGE

- Male bobcats have a larger territory (25-30 square miles) than females (5 square miles).

- Cougars are much larger than bobcats, and their tracks are twice as big. Cougars have very long tails, black tips on the ends of their ears and tail, and solid colored tan bodies.

- A Canada lynx is bigger than a bobcat and smaller than a cougar. They have lighter fur and bigger ear tufts and paws. Lynx are rare in Michigan, and are only found in some parts of the Upper Peninsula.

Coyote

(Canis latrans)

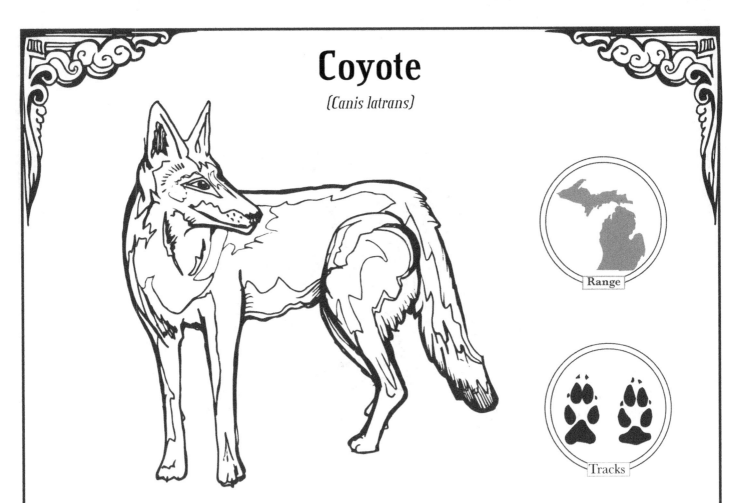

Range

Tracks

ABOUT: Coyotes are smart, social nocturnal canines. They are light brown with a white throat, pointed ears, and a bushy tail. Coyotes bark and yip like dogs and make howling sounds that can be heard for long distances.

SIZE: Length: 3 to 3.5 ft. Tail: 12 to 15in. Height: 2 ft. Weight: 20 to 40 lbs.

DIET: Coyotes are omnivores that will eat just about anything including small mammals, fruit, insects, leaves, human trash, and chickens.

SCAT: Length: 4 in. Diameter: 0.5 in. Their cylindrical scat is tapered and rope-like, and can contain fur and bones. They use scat to mark their territory, and it is often found at trail crossings and on the side of the road. Large piles of coyote scat are called latrines.

TRACKS & SIGNS: Front feet: 2.5 x 2 in. Hind feet: 2.25 x 1.75 in. Canine tracks are longer than they are wide, with one lobe on the front and two on the rear. Domestic dog tracks are usually rounder with blunt nails.

HABITAT: Coyotes live in forests, fields, swamps, and farms. They are very adaptable and are found in cities and neighborhoods. Their dens are usually in riverbanks, tree roots, or under rocks, and can be up to 30 feet long.

Coyotes hunt rodents in the winter by jumping to break through the snow.

LIFE CYCLE

In early spring, female coyotes give birth to 4 to 6 pups in a small chamber at the end of their den. The pups open their eyes after 10 days and are weaned after one month. Males leave their dens when they are about six months old, and female pups stay with their parents to form a pack. Coyotes are active year-round in Michigan. Their lifespan is 5-10 years.

NATURE KNOWLEDGE

- Coyotes can run up to 40 mph, and jump as high as 13 feet.

- Wolves are more social than coyotes, and rely heavily on the structure of their pack.

- Coyotes are larger than foxes and smaller than wolves.

- Coyotes and American badgers will sometimes work together to chase rodents out of their burrows.

North American Porcupine

(Erethizon dorsatum)

Range

Tracks

ABOUT: Porcupines are large, nocturnal, solitary rodents. Their dark brown bodies are covered with sharp spines that protect them from predators. The quills are all different sizes, some up to three inches long. Each North American porcupine has about 30,000 quills. Porcupines are very vocal and communicate through grunts and groans.

SIZE: Length: 20 to 36 in. Tail: 6 to 12 in. Height: 1 ft. Weight: 7 to 40 lb.

DIET: Herbivores, they eat tree bark, sticks, pine needles, tree buds, fruit, and leaves.

SCAT: Length: .5-1 in. Porcupine scat is pellets that are pill shaped with a curved end. It can be found by den entrances and underneath trees.

TRACKS & SIGNS: Front feet: 2.25 x 1.5 in. Hind feet: 3.25 x 2 in. They have a visible tail drag mark between their tracks. Other signs are claw marks on trees and freshly chewed small sticks.

HABITAT: Porcupines are excellent climbers and live in coniferous, deciduous, and mixed forests. They sleep in dens in hollow logs, large trees, and under rocks.

LIFE CYCLE

During mating season, male porcupines make loud vocalizations while using their quills as weapons to fight with other males. Females have one baby porcupine each spring that stays with them until fall. North American porcupines do not hibernate, but they do sleep a lot and stay near their den in the winter. Their lifespan is 5 to 15 years.

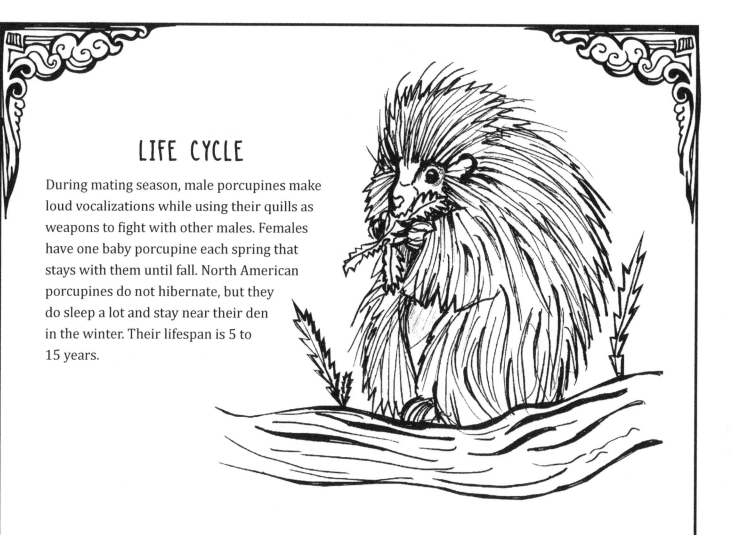

NATURE KNOWLEDGE

• Porcupine quills are modified hairs coated with a hard substance called keratin. Human fingernails are also made out of keratin.

• Porcupines have antibiotics in their skin that protect them from infection when they fall and poke themselves with their own quills.

• Young porcupines are born with soft quills that harden in a few hours. Throughout their life, new quills are constantly growing in to replace lost ones.

• Long claws and hairless palms help porcupines to climb trees. They stab the quills on their tail into tree branches to steady themselves.

Northern Raccoon

(Procyon lotor)

Range

Tracks

ABOUT: Northern raccoons are grey with a black facemask and a ringed tail. They are smart and curious and use their front paws, which look like human hands, to open containers and zippers. Raccoons are mostly nocturnal and solitary. They make snarls, purrs, whimpers, hisses, and screams.

SIZE: Length: 2 to 2.5 ft. Tail: 7 to 16 in. Height: 9 to 12 in. Weight: 12 to 30 lbs.

DIET: Raccoons are opportunistic omnivores that become easily addicted to people food. They eat crayfish, rodents, fruit, eggs, fish, amphibians, insects, carrion, and garbage.

SCAT: Length: 2 in. Diameter: 0.75 in. Their scat is tubular with blunt ends and is often found in piles.

TRACKS & SIGNS: Front feet: 2.75 x 1.5 in. Hind feet: 4 x 2 in. Raccoon tracks are hand-shaped with five fingers and small nails. Lots of small holes in your yard can be a sign of raccoons digging up insects at night.

HABITAT: Raccoons are very tolerant of human activity and can adapt to almost all habitats. They make their dens in hollow trees or underground burrows.

LIFE CYCLE

Each May, 3 to 6 raccoon kits are born that open their eyes after three weeks. In the fall, juvenile males leave to find their own home range and females stay near their mothers. Their thick fur allows them to be active year-round. Their lifespan is 2 to 10 years.

NATURE KNOWLEDGE

• Raccoons have nimble fingers and a very good sense of touch. They can untie knots and open coolers, doors, jars, and tents.

• Bare soles and palms help raccoons to climb trees quickly. They can run up to 15 miles per hour and are strong swimmers.

• Raccoons have been known to eat at bird feeders and break into chicken coops. Do not feed raccoons; it only makes them want to beg for people food instead of finding their own food.

Northern River Otter

(Lontra canadensis)

Tracks

Range

ABOUT: Northern river otters are smart and playful members of the mustelid family. They have dark brown bodies with a light brown face, big whiskers, short legs, and a long thick tail. They are semi-aquatic, and active day and night. River otters are very social and use chirps, purrs, squeaks, snorts, and whistles to communicate to each other.

SIZE: Length: 2.5 to 3.5 ft. Tail: 11 to 20 in. Height: 2 ft. Weight: 10 to 30 lb. (males are larger)

DIET: Otters are carnivores that eat fish, frogs, insects, eggs, turtles, small mammals, mollusks, crustaceans, and water birds.

SCAT: Length: 3 in. Diameter: 0.75 in. River otter scat is used as a scent symbol for other otters. Short round scat segments often contain fish scales and crawfish bones and are found on river banks. Otters leave piles of scat on trails that cross between bodies of water.

TRACKS & SIGNS: Front feet: 3.25 x 4 in. Hind feet: 3 x 3.5 in. Tracks can be found in mud and sand near water. They have partially webbed feet with five toes and claws. When otters enter into the water, they leave an impression called a slide in mud or snow that can be up to 25 feet long.

HABITAT: Otters live on the banks of lakes, rivers, and ponds. They make their dens in old burrows, hollow logs, or holes under tree roots and rocks.

LIFE CYCLE

Otters line a nest chamber at the end of their den with leaves, hair, grass, and moss. They have many different tunnel entrances, including one underwater. Adult females give birth each spring to 1 to 6 pups. Babies open their eyes after one month, are weaned after three months, and stay with their mother for up to a year. Male otters are solitary, and females are more social. They are active year-round. Their lifespan is 7 to 20 years.

River otters are playful even in the winter, and slide through snow to the water.

NATURE KNOWLEDGE

• Northern river otters can completely close their nostrils and ears to keep water out. They can stay under water for up to eight minutes.

• When hunting in muddy river bottoms, their long thick whiskers help them to sense movement.

• The fur of northern river otters has been highly valued by people for hundreds of years. Their pelts are rated 100% on the fur quality scale, because of how thick and waterproof they are.

Red Fox

(Vulpes vulpes)

Range

Tracks

ABOUT: Red foxes are smart, solitary, nocturnal members of the canine family. They are orange-red with black legs and a light face. Their bushy tail has a white tip, their ears are outlined in black, and their eyes are yellow. Red foxes communicate using facial expressions, scent markings, barks, and yelps.

SIZE: Length: 22 to 24 in. Tail: 13 to 17 in. Height: 15 to 16 in. Weight: 7 to 15 lbs.

DIET: Omnivores, they eat rodents, fruit, rabbits, insects, snakes, birds, worms, and carrion.

SCAT: Length: 3 to 6 in. Diameter: 0.5 in. Their cylindrical, segmented scat has tapered ends and often includes hair and bones. It is usually deposited on top of a log or rock to mark their territory.

TRACKS & SIGNS: Front and hind feet: 2.5 in x 2 in. The tracks of red foxes are a triangular shape with four-clawed toes. The rear foot often lands on top of where the front foot stepped. Entrances to fox dens are marked with dirt mounds and scat deposits.

HABITAT: Red foxes are found in almost every habitat in Michigan, and have adapted to human neighborhoods and farmlands. They make dens in hollow logs, abandoned burrows, or under rocks.

LIFE CYCLE

Female foxes give birth to 1 to 10 kits in early spring that open their eyes after 10 days. Both male and female red foxes bring food to their young until they leave the den in the fall. Red foxes are active year-round. Their lifespan is 5 to 10 years.

Red fox kits begin to play outside their den at about a month old.

NATURE KNOWLEDGE

• Red foxes can run up to 45 miles per hour and jump seven feet high.

• The most widely distributed canine in the world, there are 46 subspecies of red foxes ranging across Europe, Asia, Northern Africa, Australia, and North America. In some regions where they have been introduced, they are considered invasive.

• For hundreds of years, red foxes have been hunted and farmed for their beautiful fur. It takes 11 to 18 foxes to make one coat.

• Foxes will raid chicken coops. Never feed a fox, because it will learn to beg and approach humans.

Virginia Opossum

(Didelphis virginiana)

Tracks

Range

ABOUT: Virginia opossums are solitary nocturnal marsupials. They are grey with white heads, small ears, and a long pink tail. Virginia opossums are the only marsupial that lives in the United States. Marsupials are a kind of mammal that gives birth to underdeveloped young that must live in their mother's pouch for several months. Virginia opossums communicate using scent markings, and by making hissing and growling sounds.

SIZE: Length: 25 to 30 in. Tail: 10 to 20 in. Height: 6 to 10 in. Weight: 4 to 14 lbs.

DIET: Omnivores and scavengers, they eat roadkill, invertebrates, small animals, fruit, seeds, and human garbage.

SCAT: Length: 1 to 3 in. Diameter: 0.5 in. Opossum scat is firm with a pointed end. It looks a lot like the feces of a house cat.

TRACKS & SIGNS: Front feet: 2 x 2 in. Hind feet: 2.5 x 2.25 in. The front track has five fingers, and the rear track has four fingers plus an opposing thumb that points toward the body. A thin, tail drag mark is usually visible. Opossums may tear apart garbage cans and break into chicken coops.

HABITAT: Virginia opossums are very adaptable and found in forests, wetlands, meadows, cities, towns, and farms. They make their dens in hollow trees, buildings, and abandoned burrows.

LIFE CYCLE

When 2 to 13 opossum young are born each spring, they are the size of a lima bean. They are pink and tiny and helpless and cannot hear or see. They crawl through their mother's fur and into her external pouch where they live and nurse for two months. They then ride on her back until they are almost four months old. They are active year-round, even on cold winter days. Their lifespan is 3-5 years.

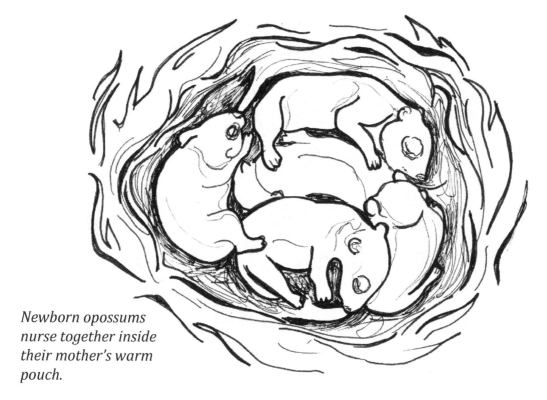

Newborn opossums nurse together inside their mother's warm pouch.

NATURE KNOWLEDGE

• When opossums are scared, they "play dead." They lie down very still, stick out their tongues, and give off a bad smell. They can continue looking dead for up to six hours to trick predators that are only interested in catching food that is alive.

• Many baby opossums do not even survive the trip to the pouch, and only about 40% live to become independent.

• Opossums are mostly terrestrial, but their semi-prehensile tails help them to balance on tree branches.

White-tailed Deer

(Odocoileus virginianus)

Range

Tracks

ABOUT: White-tailed deer are very common in Michigan. They are brown with long white tails that stick up when they run. Deer live in family groups, and only males have antlers. Females are called does, babies are called fawns, and males are called bucks. Deer grunt, sniff, bellow, wheeze, and bleat to communicate.

SIZE: Length: 5 to 7 ft. Tail: 6 to 11 in. Height: 6 to 7.75 ft. Weight: 125 to 225 lbs. (males are larger)

DIET: Deer are herbivores that eat grasses, leaves, mushrooms, berries, fruit, bark, shoots, and acorns, They especially love to feed from vegetable gardens and fruit orchards.

SCAT: Length: 0.5 in. Diameter: 0.6 in. White-tailed deer scat is usually oval-shaped dark pellets found in piles.

TRACKS & SIGNS: Front and hind feet: 3.5 to 5.5 x 2 in. The length of deer tracks varies in size depending on the age of the deer. Signs that deer have been in an area include branches ripped off trees, trampled plants, rubbed off sections of bark, antler velvet in late summer, and narrow trails worn down through the woods.

HABITAT: White-tailed deer are found in all habitats throughout Michigan, including forests, swamps, fields, sand dunes, and neighborhoods.

LIFE CYCLE

In late spring, female deer have 1 to 3 babies. They have white spots that help them camouflage with the dappled sunlight of the forest. Fawns lay still and hidden for four weeks until they can follow their mothers. Females stay with their mothers for two years and males for one. They are active year-round. Their lifespan is 2 to 10 years.

NATURE KNOWLEDGE

• White-tailed deer can run up to 35 miles per hour for short distances, and are surprisingly good swimmers.

• Deer are a valuable economic resource to the people of Michigan. There are no longer as many large predators in the state as there once was, and deer have become overpopulated. Deer hunting season helps to control population numbers, and feeds local people with a healthy meat called venison.

• Bucks have bones that grow out of their skulls called antlers. The antlers are covered with a soft velvety skin that is shed once they have reached their full size. Every winter after mating season, the antlers fall off and become an important source of calcium for rodents.

Mammal Activities

MAKE ART: Deer Antlers

- Horns and antlers are different. Horns stay on for life, and antlers fall off and regrow each year. Make your own antlers by tracing your hands on a piece of construction paper, or an old cereal box.
- Cut them out and decorate them to make your own personalized deer antlers.
- Make a headband by stapling two strips of construction paper together to fit around the top of your head.
- Staple your antlers onto your headband.

PLAY GAMES: Michigan Park Ranger Tag

- Choose 1 to 3 players to be Michigan park rangers that stand in the middle of the playing field.
- The rest of the players choose a Michigan animal to be, and stand in a forward-facing line at the edge of the playing field. Pick an animal that you know about. You do not need to tell anyone else what your animal is.
- The park rangers decide together what they would like to research. They call out an animal characteristic such as: "mammal," or "climbs trees," or "aquatic," or "herbivore," and so on.
- Players whose chosen animal has that characteristic, attempt to run to the other end of the playing field without getting tagged.
- If you are tagged, you magically become a park ranger.
- Continue play until 1 to 3 people are left untagged. They become the new ranger(s), and everyone else starts over with a new animal for the next round.

EXPERIMENT WITH SCIENCE: Make Your Own Butter

• All mother mammals produce milk; and humans use cow milk to make dairy products, such as cheese, yogurt, and butter. You can make your own butter and whipped cream.

• Fill a baby food jar half way with heavy whipping cream, close the lid tightly, and shake, shake, shake.

• After about five minutes, it will turn into whipped cream.

• Keep shaking for at least another five minutes until there is a yellow ball of butter in your jar that is surrounded by liquid buttermilk.

EXPLORE NATURE: Make Plaster Tracks

• Have an adult help you to cut a two-liter soda bottle into plastic rings.

• Take the rings, a small bowl, a spoon, some plaster of Paris, and a bottle of water with you into the field.

• Look for tracks in mud and wet sand. When you find one, put a plastic ring around it and press it into the ground.

• Pour a cup of water into your bowl. Slowly stir in plaster until your mixture is about the consistency of pancake butter.

• Carefully pour the plaster into your circle to cover the track. Let it sit for at least 30 minutes.

• Gently dig out your plaster cast. Wait until it has dried completely to clean and paint it.

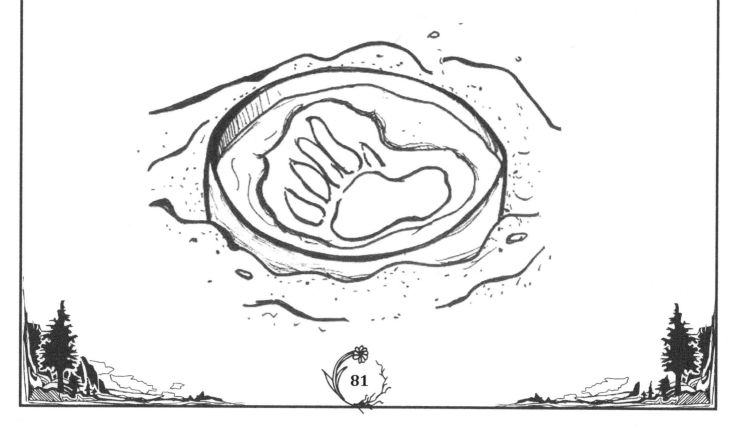

AMPHIBIAN SPECIES CHECKLIST

wasn't it was

	Date	Count	Location/Habitat
1. American toad			
2. Blanchard's cricket frog			
3. Blue-spotted salamander			
4. Boreal Chorus Frog			
5. Bullfrog ✓		~~Mishegan~~ pond	
6. Cope's tree frog ✓	2020\19\m	2	yard
7. Eastern newt			
8. Eastern red-backed salamander			
9. Eastern tiger salamander			
10. Four-toed salamander			
11. Fowler's toad			
12. Gray Tree Frog ✓		1 towlet	
13. Green frog ✓		mishegan pond	
14. Marbled salamander			
15. Mink frog			
16. Mudpuppy ✗	MM 16	marka inrid	
17. Northern leopard frog			
18. Northern spring peeper			
19. Pickerel frog			
20. Small-mouthed salamander			
21. Spotted salamander			
22. Western chorus frog			
23. Western lesser siren			
24. Wood frog	8\20\1	1	Backyard

NOTES

REPTILE SPECIES CHECKLIST

		Date	Count	Location/Habitat
1.	Blanding's turtle			
2.	Blue racer			
3.	Brown snake			
4.	Butler's garter snake	201?13	1	Backyard
5.	Common map turtle			
6.	Common musk turtle			ZOO
7.	Common snapping turtle ✓	2019	7	ZOO
8.	Copper-bellied water snake			
9.	Eastern box turtle			
10.	Eastern fox snake			
11.	Eastern garter snake			
12.	Eastern hog-nosed snake			
13.	Eastern massasauga rattlesnake			
14.	Eastern milk snake			
15.	Five-lined skink			
16.	Gray rat snake (or black rat snake)			
17.	Kirtland's snake			
18.	Northern red-bellied snake			
19.	Northern ribbon snake			
20.	Northern ring-necked snake			
21.	Northern water snake			
22.	Painted turtle			
23.	Queen snake			
24.	Red-eared slider			
25.	Six-lined racerunner			
26.	Smooth green snake			
27.	Spiny soft-shell turtle			
28.	Spotted turtle			
29.	Western fox snake			
30.	Wood turtle			

BIRD SPECIES CHECKLIST

		Date	Count	Location/Habitat
1.	American Bittern			
2.	American Crow			
3.	American Goldfinch			
4.	American Robin			
5.	Bald Eagle ✓			~~mizhyan seiye~~ lake
6.	Barred Owl			
7.	Belted Kingfisher			
8.	Black-backed Woodpecker			
9.	Black-capped Chickadee ✓	14	7	woods
10.	Black Tern			
11.	Black Vulture			
12.	Blue Jay ✓	2 0	~~~~	seiye
13.	Broad-winged Hawk			
14.	Brown-headed Cowbird			
15.	Brown Thrasher			
16.	Canada Goose	17 2021	9	oaker feld
17.	Cedar Waxwing			
18.	Common Grackle			
19.	Common Loon			
20.	Common Merganser			
21.	Common Raven			
22.	Common Starling			
23.	Common Tern			
24.	Cooper's Hawk			
25.	Dark-eyed Junco			
26.	Downy Woodpecker			
27.	Eastern Bluebird			
28.	Eastern Phoebe			
29.	Eastern Screech Owl			
30.	Eastern Towhee			

		Date	Count	Location/Habitat
31.	Evening Grosbeak			
32.	Gray Catbird			
33.	Great Blue Heron			
34.	Hairy Woodpecker			
35.	Herring Gull			
36.	House Sparrow			
37.	House Wren			
38.	King Rail			
39.	Kirtland's Warbler			
40.	Loggerhead Shrike			
41.	Mallard Duck			
42.	Mourning Dove			
43.	Northern Cardinal			
44.	Northern Flicker			
45.	Northern Harrier			
46.	Northern Mockingbird			
47.	Osprey			
48.	Peregrine Falcon			
49.	Pileated Woodpecker	✓	4	Isle woods
50.	Pine Siskin			
51.	Piping Plover			
52.	Purple Finch			
53.	Red-bellied Woodpecker			
54.	Red-breasted Nuthatch			
55.	Red Crossbill			
56.	Red-shouldered Hawk			
57.	Red-tailed Hawk			
58.	Red-winged Blackbird			
59.	Ring-billed Gull			
60.	Ruby-throated Hummingbird			

		Date	Count	Location/Habitat
61.	Ruffed Grouse			
62.	Sandhill Crane			
63.	Scarlet Tanager			
64.	Snowy Owl			
65.	Song Sparrow			
66.	Spruce Grouse			
67.	Trumpeter Swan			
68.	Tufted Titmouse			
69.	Turkey Vulture	✓	2020	3	Ski upfeild
70.	Upland Sandpiper			
71.	White-breasted Nuthatch			
72.	White-throated Sparrow			
73.	Wild Turkey	2019	1	fcld
74.	Wood Duck			
75.	Yellow-rumped Warbler			

NOTES: Make observations of birds that are not on this list here...

MAMMAL SPECIES CHECKLIST

gilt

	Date	Count	Location/Habitat
1. American badger			
2. American marten			
3. American mink			
4. American water shrew			
5. Beaver			
6. Big brown bat			
7. Black bear			
8. Bobcat			
9. Brown rat ✓	2017	1	underuvin
10. Canada lynx			
11. Cinereus shrew			
12. Cougar ✓			
13. Coyote ✓	2020	1	feld
14. Deer mouse			
15. Eastern chipmunk			
16. Eastern cottontail			
17. Eastern fox squirrel			
18. Eastern mole			
19. Elk			
20. Ermine			
21. Evening bat			
22. Fisher			
23. Gray fox			
24. Gray wolf			
25. Groundhog (woodchuck) ✓	2019	1	undedcotig
26. Hoary bat			
27. House mouse			
28. Indiana bat			
29. Least chipmunk ✓	2021	1	tree
30. Least weasel			

	Date	Count	Location/Habitat
31. Little brown bat			
32. Long-tailed weasel			
33. Meadow jumping mouse			
34. Meadow vole			
35. Moose ✓		*children home*	
36. Muskrat			
37. North American porcupine			
38. North American river otter			
39. Northern flying squirrel			
40. Northern long-eared bat			
41. Northern short-tailed shrew			
42. Pine Marten			
43. Prairie vole			
44. Raccoon ✓	*weekend*		*in my road*
45. Red bat			
46. Red fox			
47. Red squirrel			
48. Silver-haired bat			
49. Snowshoe hare			
50. Southern bog lemming			
51. Southern flying squirrel			
52. Star-nosed mole			
53. Striped skunk			
54. Thirteen-lined ground squirrel			
55. Tri-colored bat			
56. Virginia opossum			
57. White-footed mouse			
58. White-tailed deer ✓	*monday*	3	*woods*
59. Wolverine			
60. Woodland jumping mouse			
61. Woodland vole			

NATURE KNOWLEDGE DICTIONARY
Look up words that you don't know here!

A

adapt: to adjust to new or changing conditions.

adaptation: a special feature that helps an organism to survive and become better suited to a specific habitat.

aerodynamic: a shape that is designed for speed and efficiency.

amphibian: a class of animals that are cold-blooded vertebrates with moist skin.

amphisbaenids: also known as worm lizards, these reptiles look like snakes but are classified separately due to their unique skeletal structure.

aquatic: an animal that lives in or near the water for most of its life.

B

basking: when cold-blooded animals lay in the sun to raise their body temperature.

bear-safe container: a storage place that locks securely to resist bears from opening it.

breeding: producing offspring.

brood: a group of young from a specific parent.

burrow: an animal home or hiding place that is dug in the ground, leaf-litter, or snow.

C

caecilians: amphibians that look like worms, have very small eyes, and burrow under the ground.

camouflage: the ability to blend in with natural surroundings.

canine: a member of the dog family.

canopy: the highest interconnecting branches of a forest.

carapace: the hard-upper shell of a turtle.

carnivore: animals that only eat meat.

carrion: a dead animal.

cavity nest: a nest that is made in a chamber inside a tree.

Chippewa: the name of a large group of Native Americans.

class: the level of classification between phylum and order, for example: reptile and amphibian are classes.

cluster: a group of things close together.

clutch: all the eggs that are laid in a single nest.

cold-blooded: an animal with a body temperature that changes with the temperature of the surrounding air or water.

color phase: a variation in the color of an animal.

communicate: the act of transferring information.

concave: a shape that curves inward.

coniferous: a forest that is made up of mostly evergreen trees.

courtship display: a set of behaviors that animals perform during mating season.

crepuscular: animals that are most active during dawn and dusk.

crocodilian: the order that includes 23 species of alligators, crocodiles, caimans, and gharials that have long bodies with toothed jaws.

cup nest: the most common type of bird nest that is shaped like a bowl.

D

data: facts and information.

deciduous: plants that lose their leaves seasonally each year.

den: a shelter where an animal lives.

diurnal: animals that are active during the day and sleep at night.

dissect: to take apart something and examine it.

diversity: a variety of different species of plants and animals.

dormant: when the physical activity, growth, and development of a living thing are all temporarily stopped.

E

environment: the natural world.

ecosystem: a community of interconnected living organisms.

ectothermic: animals that are cold-blooded and must rely on their environment for their heat source.

endemic: a plant or animal that is only native to a certain area.

evergreen: trees that have needles or scaly leaves.

extinct: when there are not any living members of a species left on earth.

extirpated: when there are not any living members of a species within a geographic area, also known as a local extinction.

F

feline: a member of the cat family.

female: in humans, females are known as women or girls, and they are the sex of a species that can have babies as adults.

flightless: not capable of flying.

flock: a group of the same kind of birds flying, eating, or resting together.

forage: the act of searching for and collecting food.

fossil: the evidence of an organism that lived in the past.

frost-line: the lowest depth that the soil freezes at in the winter.

G

glucose: a simple sugar found inside living organisms that is used as an energy source.

glycerol: a sugar alcohol that is used as an anti-freeze in hibernating amphibians.

Great Lakes: the largest group of freshwater lakes in the world including: Lake Michigan, Lake Superior, Lake Huron, Lake Erie, and Lake Ontario.

guidebook: a book that contains educational information on a specific subject.

NATURE KNOWLEDGE DICTIONARY

H

habitat: the place where an animal lives, including food, water, shelter and space

hatchlings: a baby animal when it first comes out of an egg.

herbivore: an animal that eats plants.

herpetologist: a scientist that studies reptiles and amphibians.

hibernate: when an animal is in an inactive state during the winter, typically late October to late March in Michigan.

home-range: an area that an animal lives in.

I

incubate: when a bird sits on an egg to keep it warm so that it will hatch.

indicator species: a species that shows the health of an ecosystem through its presence, absence, or well-being.

insectivore: an animal that eats mostly insects.

internal: within the body.

invertebrate: an animal without a backbone.

K

keystone species: an animal that is very important to the rest of the species in the environment where it lives.

L

lake: a body of open water that is surrounded by land.

larva (larval): an immature animal or insect before it goes through metamorphosis, for example, tadpoles and caterpillars are larvae.

leaf-litter: a thick layer of decomposing leaves on the forest floor.

lifespan: the average amount of years that an animal lives.

litter: a group of young animals born to a single mother at one time.

M

male: in humans, a male is known as a man or a boy.

mammal: a class of warm-blooded animals with hair or fur that feed milk to their young.

marsupial: a non-placental mammal from the order Marsupialia whose young must finish development within their mother's pouch.

mate: one of a pair of animals.

mating season: the time of year that an animal reproduces.

mature forest: a forest of old trees that have reached their average height.

maturity: when an animal reaches an age that it can have babies.

metabolism: an internal process that produces energy in animals.

metamorphosis: when an animal's body changes shape completely as part of their life cycle.

NATURE KNOWLEDGE DICTIONARY

migrate: the process of moving from one place to another at a certain time of year to find food, have young, or adjust to weather changes.

mixed forest: a forest containing both evergreen and deciduous trees.

mole salamander: a group of large terrestrial salamanders that are endemic to North America, and have a larval stage called an axolotl.

molt: the process of shedding skin or feathers.

mustelid: a member of the Mustelidae family which includes otters, weasels, ferrets, skunks, badgers, wolverines, and martens.

N

native: a plant or animal that is originally from an area.

nocturnal: an animal that is active at night and sleeps during the day.

nutrients: the food or other substance that provides the nourishment for life.

O

observation: the activity of watching animals to learn more about them.

omnivore: an animal that eats both plants and animals.

opportunistic: the act of taking advantage of any available situation.

ovoviviparous: a process in some reptiles and fish that involves eggs hatching within the body so that young are born alive.

P

pellet: regurgitated undigested parts of a bird's food.

peninsula: a section of land that is surrounded by water on three sides.

permanent: existing for a long time without much change

phase: a part of the process of development.

pheromone: a chemical substance that some animals release to communicate by smell with other animals of the same species.

plastron: the lower shell of a turtle.

platform nest: a bird nest that is relatively flat in shape and can be located on the ground or in a tree.

plumage: a bird's feathers.

pond: a small body of water.

predator: an animal that catches and eats other animals for food.

prehensile tail: a tail that can wrap around objects.

prey: an animal that is eaten by another animal.

Q

quill: the hollow spine of a porcupine or the hollow center of a feather

NATURE KNOWLEDGE DICTIONARY

R

raptor: a group of birds including: eagles, falcons, owls, hawks, and kites, that catch their food with their feet that are known as talons.

regurgitate: feed undigested food to offspring.

reintroduce: the act of releasing a group of a specific species into its former habitat.

reproduce: to have babies, which is also known as producing offspring.

reptile: cold-blooded vertebrates that are members of the class Reptilia and include snakes, lizards, turtles, crocodilians, the tuatara, and amphisbaenians.

retract: to be drawn back in.

river: a moving body of water that flows down a slope towards a lake or sea.

rodent: mammals in the class Rodentia that have large front teeth that continue to grow, so they must chew on things to wear them down, including: mice, rats, squirrels, beavers, porcupines, hamsters, and their relatives.

roost: the place where a bird settles for the night.

S

scat: the word for animal poop.

scavenger: an animal that eats dead and decaying animals or plants.

scientific method: a systematic procedure used in natural science.

seed disperser: an animal that moves seeds away from the parent plant.

shallow: not very deep.

shed: when a reptile changes its skin as it grows.

silhouette: the shape that a bird makes in the sky while soaring.

soaring: the act of staying in the air without the flapping of wings.

solitary: an animal that lives by itself.

species: a group of similar living things that can reproduce.

species of special concern: an uncommon species that may become threatened or endangered if it is not protected and monitored.

T

talons: the large hooked claws of raptors.

temperate: a region where the weather changes seasonally from warm to cold.

terrestrial: an animal that lives on land for most of its life.

territory: an area of land that an animal lives in and protects, either by itself, in a pair, or with a group.

torpor: when an animal's body temperature and metabolism are very low, and the animal is inactive throughout a season.

tree cavity: a hole in a tree trunk or branch.

tuatara: a reptile that is lizard-like, but is actually related to dinosaurs and is only found living on small islands off the coast of New Zealand.

NATURE KNOWLEDGE DICTIONARY

U

undergrowth: a layer of short plants in a forest that don't grow as tall as the trees.

understory: small trees and shrubs that form the layer of forest in between the canopy and the ground cover.

urinate: to pee.

V

vegetation: plants.

venom: a poison that is made by an animal's body and injected into their prey.

venomous: an animal that has a gland that produces poison.

vertebrate: an animal with a backbone.

vocalization: the act of making sounds that are usually used to communicate with others of the same species.

vocal sac: a loose flap of skin on the throat that can be blown up like a balloon to make a loud sound.

W

warm-blooded: an animal with a body temperature that stays the same, regardless of environmental temperature change.

weaned: when a young mammal stops being dependent on its mother's milk and eats other food.

wetland: a habitat that is wet most of the time, such as a swamp or a marsh.

wildlife: wild animals that are native to a region.

wingspan: the length of a bird's wings measured from tip to tip.

woodlands: an area of land that is covered with trees.

Please Note: Definitions provided are in relation to the naturalist use of the word in regards to the content of this book.

ACKNOWLEDGMENTS

I would like to acknowledge several influential people that have made this project possible. First and foremost, my incredible team: Aimé Merizon, Patrick B. Bradley, and Anna Bazyl.

This book has finally gone to print because of the support of Aimé Merizon and the Benzie Conservation District (BCD). By contributing her graphic design skills to this project, Aimé pieced together an unfinished dream into an assembled product.

Without the vision and creativity of Patrick B. Bradley, this project would never have evolved into what it is today. Patrick provided the original illustrations including: the borders, main animal pictures, tracks, and range maps. His realistic drawings and detailed border scenes shaped the character of this book.

I am incredibly impressed by Anna Bazyl's talent and work ethic. She created the life-cycle, introduction, and activity drawings within the final month before publication. She brought my words to life through illustrations that are both beautiful and educational.

Thank you to everyone that contributed to the Kickstarter project! You provided the extra push needed to get this book published. An extra special thanks to our Super Sponsors, who offered generous financial help to make this publication a reality. I am very appreciative that, out of all the good work there is to support in the world, you chose to back ***Michigan Wildlife: A Coloring Field Guide*** with your hard-earned dollars.

Thank you, from the bottom of my heart:

Birchard Ohlinger

Debbie Chase

Granny Franny Holly and Grandpa Rick DeZeeuw

Luette Frost

Rory and Sean Carlson

William L. Huntington, IV

I am eternally grateful to my parents, Diana Hooyman and Steven Fernand, who have consistently encouraged me to follow my dreams. And to my siblings, Eliza Fernand, Maggie Hooyman, and Patrick Hooyman Jr. and my niece, Daisy Jean Hooyman, who each inspire me with their own artistic abilities.

I am humbled by the greatness of the women who were my grandmothers, and who played important roles in shaping my life before they left this world. Jeanne Pettengill, who inspired so much of me with her love of birds, photography, and travel. And Leola Hereford whose strength, independence, and financial support have impacted every aspect of my current path in life.

I am continually in awe of the truly amazing Avalon Theisen of Conserve It Forward, whom provided the Human Frog Chorus activity for this book. Avalon has followed her passion for conservation since a young age with a drive and determination that is unparalleled.

I am thankful for all the encouragement and help that I had editing this manuscript from my great friends and mentors: Amy Ross, Emily Schaller, George Heinrich, Jason Rusch, Patrick Hooyman, and Susan Koenig.

Thank you to the families that have supported me by bringing your children to Nature Explorers classes, and to those that purchase this book. You are truly nurturing the innate desire in your child to learn about the natural world, and providing an important framework for their future. Appreciation and compassion for nature are rooted in curiosity and understanding, inevitably leading towards conservation. Young naturalists are the future of this earth, and I am thankful to all Nature Explorers out there, young and old. We are making a difference.

Book proceeds will go towards creating a permanent Nature Explorers classroom space in Benzonia, Michigan.

Forever grateful,

Amalia Celeste Fernand

REFERENCES

Cox, D. J. (1990). Black Bear. San Francisco, CA: Chronicle Books.

Behler, J. L. & King, F. W. (1979). The Audubon Society Field Guide to North American Reptiles and Amphibians. Syracuse, NY: Chanticleer Press Inc.

Burt, W.H. & Grossenheider, R.P. (1980). A Field Guide to the Mammals, North America, North of Mexico. Boston, MA: Houghton Mifflin Company.

Fichter, G.S. (1993). A Golden Junior Guide: Turtles, Toads, and Frogs. Racine, WI: Western Publishing Company Inc.

Gillette, J. (1984). Coat Pocket Bird Book. Lansing, MI: Two Peninsula Press.

Harding, J.H. & Mifsud, D.A. (2017). Amphibians and Reptiles of the Great Lakes Region, Revised Edition. Ann Arbor, MI: University of Michigan Press.

Johnson, F. (1973). The Foxes. Washington, DC: National Wildlife Federation.

Kobasa, P. A. (Ed.). (2006). Cardinals and Other Songbirds. Chicago, IL: World Book Inc.

Latimer, J. P. & Nolting, K. S. (1999). Peterson Field Guide for Young Naturalists: Backyard Birds. Boston, MA: Houghton Mifflin Company.

Parker, S. (2004). See-through Reptiles. Philadelphia, PN: Running Press Book Publishers.

Patent, D. H. (1989). Wild Turkey, Tame Turkey. New York, NY: Clarion Books.

Robbins, C. S., Brunn, B. & Zim, H.S. (2001). Birds of North America, a Golden Field Guide from St. Marten's Press. New York, NY: St. Martin's Press.

Sibley, D. A. (2010). Sibley's: Waterbirds of the Great Lake Region. Wilton, NH: Steven M. Lewers & Associates.

Tekiela, S. (1999). Birds of Michigan Field Guide. Cambridge, MN: Adventure Publications Inc.

Tekiela, S. (2005). Mammals of Michigan Field Guide. Cambridge, MN: Adventure Publications Inc.

Tekiela, S. (2004). Reptiles & Amphibians of Michigan Field Guide. Cambridge, MN: Adventure Publications Inc.

Zim, H. S. & Hoffmeister, D.F. (1987). A Golden GuideMammals. New York, NY: Golden Books.